Every Pregnant Woman's Guide to Preventing Premature Birth

A Program for Reducing the Sixty Proven Risks That Can Lead to Prematurity

Barbara Luke, Sc.D., M.P.H., R.N., R.D.

TIMES BOOKS

RANDOM HOUSE

Library of Congress Cataloging-in-Publication Data

Luke, Barbara.
Every pregnant woman's guide to preventing premature
birth: a program for reducing the sixty proven risks that
can lead to prematurity / Barbara Luke.
p.   cm.
Includes bibliographical references and index.
ISBN 0-8129-2472-X
1. Labor, Premature—Prevention—Popular works.
I. Title.
RG649.L85   1995
618.3'97—dc20   95-12213

Designed by Brooke Zimmer

Manufactured in the United States of America
9   8   7   6   5   4   3   2
FIRST EDITION

Every Pregnant Woman's Guide to Preventing Premature Birth

*To Dr. Mandan Farahati,
wife, mother, friend, and obstetrician:
in recognition and appreciation of the
many lives she has touched during
her long and caring career*

Acknowledgments

I would like to acknowledge the following individuals who were important in the conception and development of this book. First of all, I would like to thank Professor Emile Papiernik, who headed the French program from which many of the concepts of this book were based; Dr. George Wilbanks, for his encouragement during its development; and Kit Ward, my literary agent, for her idea development and constant support. I also want to thank Delores Miller and Gladys Medina-Cruz for their readings of earlier versions and their helpful comments and encouragement; I also want to thank Delores for typing the many tables in this book. A special thanks goes to Dr. Harold Bigger and the nursing staff of the Special Care Nursery at Rush-Presbyterian–St. Luke's Medical Center for their help in obtaining newborn footprints. Special thanks also goes to Ms. Kristen Wienandt, for her beautiful drawings and her translations of the newborn footprints.

At Times Books/Random House, I would like to thank Executive Editor Elizabeth Rapoport for her vision and belief in the importance of this book; her editorial assistant, Louise Braverman, for her close attention to details; Robbin Schiff for the cover design; and Naomi Osnos for the layout. I would also like to thank Patricia Romanowski for her superb copy editing.

Last, and most important, I want to thank my parents; my son, Peter Martin Wissel; and my sister, Dianne Pearson; for their faith in all of my work and their enduring love.

Foreword

More than one out of ten U.S. births is premature, and
the rate has been gradually increasing over the last fifteen years. Prematurity and its inherent complications
for mother and infant are a major cause of infant death
in the first year of life. Those that survive may be adversely affected in growth and development. The cost
in family stress and health-care dollars is staggering.

Some of the many factors related to a woman's having a premature infant have been researched exten-
sively and are well known; others are not as easily
understood. Further factors will be discovered as research continues. However, a number of situations
have been identified as risk factors; understanding
them and taking appropriate action can lessen the
chance of prematurity. Some of these are nutrition,
medical history, family history, lifestyle, exercise, and
work conditions. The French national prematurity pro-

gram, started in 1971, has applied some of the clearly related data on these risk factors to successfully lower the prematurity rate in France.

Dr. Barbara Luke has spent most of her career in maternal health and prematurity. She has drawn on and extended the experience from her five books, numerous articles, and her work with the French prematurity program to present in clear, concise, practical, scientifically accurate form an invaluable guide to identifying the sixty most important risk factors associated with prematurity.

The book is organized in a logical sequence of easy-to-read chapters. Appropriate, concise tables and charts are helpful, particularly the "Preventing Prematurity Checklist." The book also includes an extensive glossary of terms and a comprehensive bibliography for those who wish more details on a specific subject. These are helpful for both medical professionals and the lay public.

As a practicing obstetrician-gynecologist of many years, I believe most women want the best for their unborn children. If given the right information, they will make changes in their lives to help assure the healthiest outcome. *Every Pregnant Woman's Guide to Preventing Premature Birth* is an important contemporary book that should be recommended reading for today's pregnant women, women considering pregnancy, and all those professionals who attend the health care of women.

—George D. Wilbanks, Jr., M.D.
Professor and Chairman, Department of Obstetrics
and Gynecology, Rush Medical College,
Rush-Presbyterian–St. Luke's Medical Center,
and President, American College of Obstetricians
and Gynecologists

Contents

Preface

Premature birth is one of the leading causes of disability, which can severely limit a child's ability to fulfill his or her physical and intellectual potential. Prematurity has long been a perplexing problem for obstetricians and pregnant women alike. There is no single cause and no single solution. Many factors contribute to a woman's risk of delivering prematurely, and the same factor may not have the same effect in two different women.

Prematurity is often preventable. In France we decided to take steps to see if we could lower the rate of prematurity. Between 1971 and 1981, the French government implemented a national program to reduce perinatal-related disability, including preterm births. This program, which I directed, succeeded in lowering the prematurity rate by 52 percent (from 8.2 percent in 1972 to 3.9 percent in 1989) and the early preterm rate (births before 34 weeks' gestation) by 50 percent (from 2.4 percent in 1972 to 1.2 percent in 1989). Our program was based on the premise that the physical efforts and activities of daily life cause uterine contractions, which in turn, increase the risk of prematurity. We taught the mothers-to-be to recognize these uterine contractions and advised them to reduce their physical efforts, especially if their pregnancy was recognized as higher risk—no matter what their medical or obstetric histories.

Although the social and medical situations are different in France and the United States, several important components of this successful program could—and should—be adopted here. Pregnant women in America should be taught how to modify their daily activities to reduce physical stress, learn the signs and symptoms of preterm uterine contractions, and enjoy a reasonable work leave. Since 1928, France has had an enlightened maternity policy whereby pregnant women are entitled to work leave both before and after birth, continuation of wages and benefits, and job security for fourteen weeks, with an additional two weeks for medical reasons. Although the United States does not have such a policy, the Pregnancy Discrimination Act of 1978 and the Family and Medical Leave Act of 1993 provide important benefits for pregnant women, including work leave. *Every Pregnant Woman's Guide to Preventing Premature Birth* does adopt important components of our program as well as offer a great deal more. Geared to the unique lifestyles of American women, Dr. Luke's book explores all aspects of a woman's life to help her identify her personal risks and offers practical suggestions for reducing those risks that can be changed.

More than one out of ten births is premature in the United States—one of the highest rates of any industrialized nation. In any language and in any country, prevention is the best medicine. I wholeheartedly recommend Dr. Luke's book to every pregnant woman and her family as the "best medicine" to help ensure a healthy pregnancy.

—Emile Papiernik, M.D.
Professor of Obstetrics and Gynecology,
Head of Maternity,
Maternité Port-Royal, Paris, France

Every Pregnant Woman's Guide to Preventing Premature Birth

1

Prematurity and Its Consequences

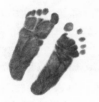

"I went into premature labor while standing on the train during the ride home one evening from work. At first I thought it was just a backache, but then the pains spread to my stomach and were worse than any menstrual cramps I had ever had. I didn't know what was happening to me, and when the train stopped, I went straight to the hospital. The doctors gave me drugs to try to stop the contractions, but within hours I gave birth to our son, Joshua. He was twelve weeks premature and weighed only two and a half pounds. He lived for two weeks connected to machines, but he died before ever leaving the hospital. I keep going over in my mind, What did I do wrong? My husband and I are both college educated, we don't drink or smoke, and I had read everything I could about pregnancy and childbirth. We had waited to have this child until we could afford a house, but now it seems so empty. His death will haunt me forever, I know."

"I will never forget the first time I saw Tracy, my daughter. My wife had gone into premature labor, and after an emergency cesarean delivery, they took Tracy to the neonatal intensive care unit. She looked so tiny and fragile inside that incubator, with tubes and bandages and all those monitors! They wouldn't let me hold her—I think I would have been afraid to, anyway. I went home that night and prayed for hours that she would live, and finally cried myself to sleep. That was one of the worst nights of my life. It was touch and go for weeks, and several times we thought we were going to lose her. She's two years old now, and she has some problems with her hearing and speech, and she's short for her age. But we are so grateful that she's alive, and every birthday is a very special occasion for us."

PREMATURITY, birth before 37 completed weeks' gestation, is one of the greatest public health problems in the United States today. Each year in the United States there are over four million births. More than one out of ten of these births is premature, or about 440,000 annually. Half of all deaths to children before their first birthday are due to pregnancy-related factors; nine out of ten of these deaths are due to prematurity and its complications.

Premature babies—preemies—are more than merely small. They are developmentally unprepared for life outside the uterus. If they survive, they are more likely to have problems with growth and development, which can result in physical and mental disabilities. For example, children who were born premature are more likely to have respiratory problems during childhood, as well as a higher incidence of learning disabilities and problems with speech, hearing, and vision. The more premature the infant, the greater the risk of physical and developmental problems during childhood.

"As a school nurse, I can always tell which children had been born prematurely and which had been born at term. Although the home environment can make up for a lot, children born prematurely generally have more chronic health problems. The more premature, the worse the problems. Some seem to improve with age, like height and weight, but others seem to persist, like difficulties with vision and hearing. Many of those who were very premature have major learning problems in school, as well."

Maturity is not the only factor influencing how healthy your baby will be at birth and during infancy: Birthweight is also very important. Babies who were "small-for-gestational age (SGA)" or "intrauterine-growth-retarded" (IUGR) have not grown as well as they should have before birth (see Figure 1). Intrauterine growth retardation, or being less than the 10th percentile for gestational age, is associated with increased risks of death during the newborn period, and among survivors, increased illnesses during infancy. Many of the same factors cause both prematurity and poor

Figure 1.
Evaluating Birthweight
for Gestational Age

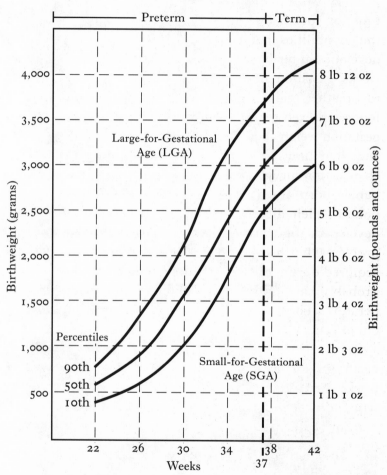

Infants with birthweights less than the 10th percentile for their gestational age (SGA) are at increased risk of death during the neonatal period, or if they survive, illnesses during infancy. Examples would be a 34-week infant weighing 1,500 grams or a 36-week infant weighing 2,000 grams.

growth before birth. When an infant is both premature and growth-retarded, the risks of death or subsequent disability are greatly increased.

Every week prematurity is prevented buys valuable time for your baby to grow and mature, and increases the possibilities that he or she will be healthy and well-developed at birth (see Table 1). At 24, 28, 32, 36, or 40 weeks' gestation, newborns have very different abilities to breathe, maintain their body temperature, digest food, and even see and hear. Babies born at 24 weeks' gestation weigh about 1 pound, their eyes are still shut, and their lungs are only minimally developed. Their chances for survival are about one in ten. In contrast, babies born at 36 weeks' gestation weigh about 5½ pounds, their digestion, sight, and vision are all well developed, they may or may not have any respiratory problems, but because they lack the body fat normally acquired during the last month of pregnancy, they will probably have difficulty maintaining their body temperature. Their chances of survival are probably nine out of ten.

Respiratory distress syndrome (abbreviated as RDS) occurs in about 11 percent of infants born before 32 weeks' gestation, compared to about 4 percent of infants born before 37 weeks' gestation, and less than 1 percent of infants born after 37 weeks' gestation. RDS occurs when the lungs are underdeveloped and collapse instead of functioning normally to exchange air with each breath. Likewise, the more premature the infant, the more likely the need for machines to assist in breathing. Nearly 14 percent of infants born before 32 weeks' gestation need to be put on ventilators to breathe, compared to 4 percent of infants born before

Table 1. *Growth and Development Before Birth*

Weeks' Gestation	Average Length	Average Weight	Physical Characteristics	Survival	Chances of Normal Development
24	12"	1¼–1½ lb	• Distinctive footprints and fingerprints • Eyebrows and eyelashes recognizable	10%	40%
26	13"	2–2¼ lb	• Skin is thin and shiny • Eyelids begin to part and eyes open	20%	60%
28	14"	2½–3 lb	• Moves arms and legs vigorously • Eyelids are open; cries weakly	50%	80%
30	15"	3–3½ lb	• May suck his/her thumb • Responds to stimuli (sound, light)	75%	85%
32	16"	3½–4 lb	• Skin is still red and wrinkled • Toenails present	85%	90%
34	17"	4½–5 lb	• Can see and hear • Lungs may still be immature	95%	95%
36	18"	5½–6½ lb	• Still lacking in body fat • May be anemic and need iron	99%	99%
38–40	19"–20"	7–8½ lb	• Round, plump arms and legs • Strong cry, attentive when awake	99%	99%

37 weeks' gestation and less than 1 percent of infants born after 37 weeks' gestation.

"My son Jimmy was born at thirty weeks' gestation. The nurses wheeled me down to the neonatal intensive care unit in a wheelchair so I could get my first look at him a few hours after I gave birth. I don't know why, but I was so surprised to see him hooked up to so many machines and monitors. I guess I just expected that he'd just be small. The ventilator really scared me— the tube seemed half as big as Jimmy. With all those tubes he couldn't even cry like a normal newborn. I couldn't hold him for weeks, until he was taken off the ventilator. He was in the intensive care unit for two months, and those were the longest two months of my life."

The footprints in Figure 2 are lifesize, to show you how small and fragile these premature infants really are. Special precautions must be taken for premature babies, including administering oxygen, placing them in heated incubators, feeding them special dietary formulas, muffling extraneous sound and light, and protecting their fragile skin. During recent years, there have been great advances in the care of these infants and improvements in their survival rates, but despite modern technology, there is no substitute for full-term gestation.

Prematurity is on the rise in the United States. It has increased by about 20 percent since 1980. What causes prematurity? Why is it increasing? Are all women at equal risk? Prematurity is a complex, universal problem, with no single cause and no single solution. It occurs in every city, state, region, and country on the face

Figure 2

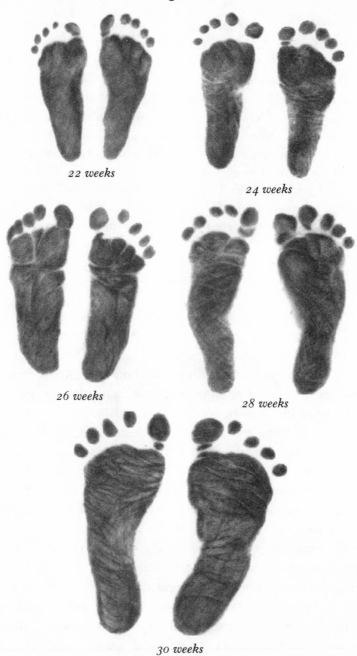

22 weeks

24 weeks

26 weeks

28 weeks

30 weeks

Actual-Size Footprints of Fetuses Week by Week

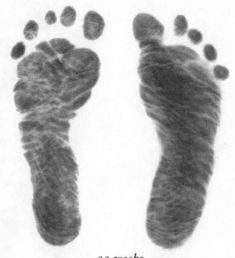

32 weeks

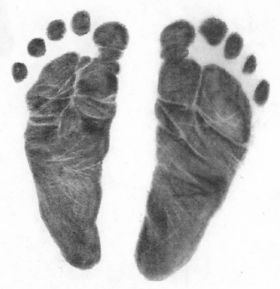

34 weeks

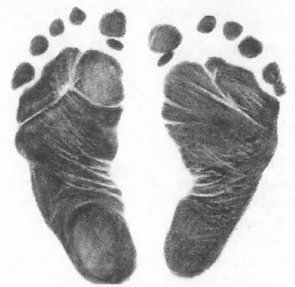

36 weeks

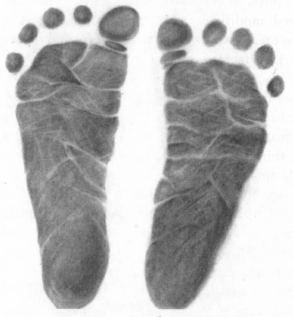

38 weeks

of the earth. Many factors contribute, and what poses a risk for you may have little effect on your neighbor. Perhaps one of the strongest risk factors is a prior premature birth. For example, if your first pregnancy ended in a premature birth, your risk of delivering prematurely again is increased more than threefold; if both your first and second births ended prematurely, your risk for your third pregnancy is increased nearly sevenfold. *All women of all races and social classes can potentially deliver prematurely, and their infants can suffer from the effects of being born too early and too small.*

Each woman brings a unique set of factors to each pregnancy. Some risks cannot be changed, such as your genetic background, obstetrical history, and age; these are considered nonmodifiable risks. Others, such as how much and how often you lift, carry, stand, or make other physical efforts, can be changed. These are considered modifiable risks. Traditional obstetric care doesn't teach women how to recognize and reduce their own risk factors during pregnancy. Most women, therefore, do not realize how much they really can do to reduce their risks and improve the health of their unborn babies. Most of the pregnancy books on the market focus on preparing you for labor—an event that lasts thirteen hours, on average. My focus is on the whole nine months of your pregnancy: a short-term investment for the lifelong health of your child and the outcome of future pregnancies as well (see Chapter 2).

I hope this book will help you in making a careful assessment of your personal risks and a reduction of those you can. While no one can guarantee that your pregnancy will not be premature, by taking the best possible care of yourself and reducing whatever risks you can, you will greatly improve your chances of having a healthy, well-grown baby born at term.

Why should you listen to my advice? For several good reasons. I was originally trained as a nurse, and although I have gone on in research, over the past twenty-five years I have continued to work in newborn nurseries and neonatal intensive care units. About six years ago, I was in graduate school in Baltimore and working weekends in the newborn nurseries at an obstetrical hospital in Washington, D.C. When one of my fellow nursery nurses went into premature labor during a particularly hectic shift, I suddenly realized that every pregnant nurse I had ever worked with had given birth prematurely! Considering that nurses are generally well educated, well nourished, and physically fit, I wondered if it was the nature of our work that might be the real cause of prematurity. In obstetrics we always concentrate on the "traditional" risk factors as the most likely causes of prematurity—poverty, poor nutrition, lack of prenatal care, drugs, and smoking. True, these factors probably do contribute to prematurity in the United States, but only a small portion. The pregnant nurses I worked with had none of these "traditional" risk factors, but they did have a whole set of others related to their work. Several of these nurses worked twelve-hour shifts on Saturdays and Sundays so they could be home with their young children during the week. Others did double shifts (sixteen hours) to accommodate their husbands' work schedules. We all stood most of the time, walked miles every day bringing the babies back and forth to their mothers, and worked in environments that were frequently very noisy (imagine a room filled with fifty crying babies at feeding time!). Individuals working in health care must also be constantly ready to handle any emergency—a reality that can add a lot of stress to everyday work. Long hours, physical effort, fatigue, and stress all seemed to me to increase nurses' risks for prematurity.

This relationship seemed so strong and so clear to me that I began to search for studies that could provide scientific evidence to back up my intuition. My search revealed that many studies had been done, all around the world. The French had taken a particular interest in this area and had actually implemented a national program based on these scientific findings. Initiated in 1971, the French national prematurity prevention program succeeded in lowering the prematurity rate by more than 50 percent. One of the major reasons for their success was that instead of targeting specific groups of women for prevention, they educated *all* women on the factors associated with prematurity, especially the effects of physical efforts and activities in daily life that cause uterine contractions and premature labor. This program taught women how to recognize their own uterine contractions and what to do if they occurred. In addition, this program empowered women by helping them identify and modify their own risks, thereby improving their chances of having a healthy, term pregnancy.

This program was headed by Professor Emile Papiernik, an obstetrician. In 1989 I went to France to meet Dr. Papiernik and learn about his work. I told him about my experiences with my pregnant co-workers and proposed that we collaborate on a study of American nurses. He agreed, and I asked the Association of Women's Health, Obstetric, and Neonatal

Nurses (AWHONN) to let us survey their membership to study the relationship between work and prematurity. The nurses in AWHONN work in newborn nurseries, neonatal intensive care, labor and delivery, and other areas of obstetrics and gynecology. AWHONN agreed to participate in our study, and we were off! Over the next two years we worked closely with the scientists in France who had evaluated their own program in designing our survey. After two pilot surveys we finally sent out the survey to the entire membership of AWHONN, and the findings confirmed my initial observations: Standing, long hours, noise, fatigue, and stress were all strongly associated with prematurity, even when none of the "traditional" risk factors was present!

These findings, the evidence from the scientific literature, and the results of the French program are the reasons I wrote this book, and why I hope you'll take my advice. With prematurity on the rise in the United States, I felt that it was especially important for women today to reduce their "nontraditional" risk factors, those associated with physical activity and the stresses of daily life. Face it, we do work harder than our mothers did, and the stress of our lives is catching up with us and manifesting in many illnesses. Among women who are balancing work, home, and pregnancy, the price of a hectic life is also reflected by the increase in prematurity. Because of the devastating effects prematurity can have on our own lives and the lives of our children, we must make every effort to reduce the chances of it occurring. Based on many of the proven concepts and principles of the French national program and updated to include current research, this is the first and only book of its kind to present practical, scientifically sound information on the *sixty most important risk factors associated with prematurity* and *how to reduce them*. This revolutionary book will help you take stock of your home and work environments, your gynecologic and obstetrical history, and myriad other risk factors to determine your personal risks for prematurity and how to modify and reduce them.

Because pregnancy and childbirth are so common (with more than four million births in the United States each year), sometimes we tend to take it for granted. It is really a very complicated, almost magical process that happens just once for each child. Many things can go wrong, and many things are beyond our control. But there is much that you *can* do to lay a strong foundation for your child's future health. As a mother, you have a unique opportunity to make a difference in your child's life long before he or she is born. Whether this is your first pregnancy or your fifth, whether you've had a preterm birth or not, this book is important reading for you and your partner.

You are going to read a lot of numbers throughout this book, and some of them may scare you. Sometimes the best way to make a point is to simply lay out the bare facts, which are presented here, based on my review of thousands of published scientific studies. This book is based on my nearly twenty-five years of experience working with mothers, families, and thousands of newborn babies, some of whom were so small they could fit in the palm of my hand. This book begins with a questionnaire for you to answer—a starting point for your own personal assessment of your daily life. The answers to this questionnaire will pinpoint the risks currently present in your life and provide the focus for the rest of the book—how to reduce the risks you have identified. Next, we will cover the "traditional" risk factors, including family background, and gynecological, obstetrical, and medical risk factors. We will then concentrate on your home and work environments, identifying risks and offering solutions to reduce them. We will also evaluate your lifestyle risk factors (the use of alcohol, drugs, tobacco, and caffeine; recreational exercise), and nutritional risk factors. At the end of the book, I'll ask you to fill out the questionnaire again, after you've put your personal prematurity prevention program to work, so that you can see how well you've done in reducing your risks and improving your chances for a healthier pregnancy. The last chapter of the book is about pregnancy-related laws, a comparison with those in Europe, and how to make the current U.S. laws work for you.

I wish you the very best in your pregnancy. It is a magical, special time, filled with hopes, dreams, and some natural anxiety about how it will all turn out. Above all, be reassured that having a baby today is safer than at any time in history. We know more about what happens and about what can go wrong. This book will help you take positive actions to reduce some of those anxieties. Let's begin!

Your Personal Risk Assessment Questionnaire

Answer each question below as yes (1 point) or no (0 point) in either column A or B, as indicated.

	Col. A	Col. B
Family Background		
1. Do you consider yourself African-American?	yes	no
2. Were you born in the United States?	yes	no
3. Are you younger than eighteen or older than thirty-five?	yes	no
4. Is your annual household income less than $8,000 for a family of two, or less than $10,000 for a family of three?	yes	no
5. Are you a single parent?	yes	no
6. Do you have preschool children at home?	yes	no
7. Do you have more than two children at home?	yes	no
8. Do one or more elderly relatives live with you?	yes	no
Gynecological, Obstetrical, and Medical History Factors		
Before this pregnancy, have you had		
9. —any spontaneous abortions?	yes	no
10. —any induced abortions?	yes	no
11. —any preterm births?	yes	no
Were any of your previous newborns		
12. —born dead (stillborn)?	yes	no
13. —less than 5¼ pounds at birth?	yes	no
14. —dead within one month after birth?	yes	no
15. Do you have a history of infertility treatments?	yes	no

	Col. A		Col. B	

16. Did your mother take diethylstilbestrol (DES) when she was pregnant with you? — yes no
17. Is this your first pregnancy? — yes no
18. Have you given birth four or more times before? — yes no
19. Did you have any preexisting medical conditions? — yes no

Current Obstetrical Factors

20. Have you had any vaginal bleeding after twelve weeks? — yes no
21. Do you have any placental complications? — yes no
22. Have you been told you have an incompetent cervix? — yes no
23. Do you have premature rupture of the membranes (PROM)? — yes no
24. Have you had one or more vaginal infections? — yes no
25. Are you pregnant with more than one baby (multiple gestation)? — yes no

Home and Work Environment Factors

26. Do you climb stairs at home? — yes no
27. Do you do much lifting at home? — yes no
28. Do you do much carrying at home? — yes no
29. Do you do much standing at home? — yes no
30. Is your home environment noisy? — yes no
31. Do you spend much time driving (carpool, groceries, errands)? — yes no
32. Is your job high-stress or physically demanding? — yes no
33. Do you stand while commuting to and from work? — yes no
34. Do you stand most of the time at work? — yes no

		Col. *A*		*Col.* *B*	
35.	Do you do much lifting at work?			yes	no
36.	Does your job require much physical exertion?			yes	no
37.	Do you have irregular work hours?			yes	no
38.	Does your job involve shift work?			yes	no
39.	Do you work more than eight hours per day?			yes	no
40.	Do you work more than forty hours per week?			yes	no
41.	Do you become fatigued at work?			yes	no
42.	Is your work environment noisy?			yes	no
43.	Are you under a lot of stress at work?			yes	no
44.	Do you drive at work or commute to work?			yes	no

Lifestyle Factors

				Col. B	
45.	Do you drink alcohol?			yes	no
46.	Do you smoke cigarettes?			yes	no
47.	Do you drink more than two cups of coffee per day?			yes	no

If you participate in recreational exercise,

				Col. B	
48.	—do you exercise on your back or until fatigued?			yes	no
49.	—do you exercise until you perspire?			yes	no

Nutritional Historical Factors

		Col. A			
50.	Are you less than five feet tall?	yes	no		
51.	Can you pinch less than one inch of fat on your arm?	yes	no		
52.	Are you underweight for your height?	yes	no		
53.	Have you recently been dieting to lose weight?	yes	no		
54.	Have you recently had a major illness or surgery?	yes	no		

	Col. A	Col. B

Nutritional Factors in the Current Pregnancy

Have you been told that you have

55. —to eat more frequently (don't fast)?	yes	no
56. —not gained enough weight before 20 weeks?	yes	no
57. —not gained enough weight after 20 weeks?	yes	no
58. —iron-deficiency anemia?	yes	no
59. —an inadequate iron intake?	yes	no
60. —an inadequate calcium intake?	yes	no

Now add up your answers. Each "yes" answer is worth one point, and each "no" answer is worth zero points. Keep your column A and column B totals separate. Your score in column A represents your nonmodifiable risk factors, those you cannot change. Although you can't do anything about them, by recognizing that they exist, they should make you more careful about reducing those risk factors you can modify, those in column B. This book is about reducing your modifiable, column B factors. The next five chapters will discuss individual risk factors and how to reduce or eliminate them. If your score right now seems high, don't panic. There's a lot you can do to improve your profile. Remember, you'll be taking this questionnaire again at the end of the book after you have assessed your home and work environments, lifestyle, and diet and reduced those modifiable factors that you can.

But first, let's review the traditional risk factors, those that your doctor will most likely ask you about during your first office visit. While most of these risk factors are nonmodifiable, they are important to recognize.

2

*Traditional Risk Factors:
What Your Doctor Is Likely
to Ask You*

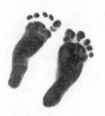

In THIS CHAPTER we're going to talk about your "traditional" risk factors, those that your doctor is likely to ask you about during your first office visit. These factors include your family background, and your gynecological, obstetrical, and medical history. These are mostly your nonmodifiable, column A, risk factors. Although you cannot change them, it is very important to be aware of them, as they increase your overall risk of prematurity. Medical histories don't make for the most exciting reading, but analyzing where you fit in this profile will help you understand your doctor's perspective. Also, if you realize that you have many of these nonmodifiable risk factors, it should encourage you to change the other risk factors that are under your control.

What is Your Racial and Ethnic Background?

To begin, let's start with your personal characteristics, what makes you uniquely you! Your racial and ethnic background are risk factors that can influence the outcome of your pregnancy, although scientists are not completely sure why. Race and ethnicity are difficult factors to measure, because they really represent a combination of biology and culture. In the United States, black women are at the highest risk for delivering prematurely (18 percent), followed by Hispanic (12 percent) and caucasian women (9 percent); Asian mothers have the lowest risk (8 percent). Recent studies have shown that even among college graduates, black women still have a higher incidence of preterm birth compared to white women (1). If you are black, even if you don't have other risk factors, you have an increased risk of delivering preterm.

Where Were You Born?

It may surprise you to learn that, for certain racial and ethnic groups, whether you were born abroad or in the United States (your nativity) also influences your risk of premature birth (2,3). The incidence of premature births is lower for women born abroad who are black, Hispanic, or Asian. Again, scientists aren't sure why nativity influences the risk of prematurity. It is probably a combination of differences in nutrition, smoking and drinking choices, health care, family resources, and other factors.

How Old Are You?

Your age is another nonmodifiable risk factor. If you are younger than eighteen years old or over thirty if this is your first pregnancy, you have an increased risk of prematurity, but for very different reasons.

Too Young?

Every year in the United States there are nearly one million pregnancies and more than 500,000 births to girls less than eighteen years of age (4). For these girls, the risks associated with becoming pregnant are both biologic and economic. Part of the biologic risk is due to the fact that many girls in this age group are still growing themselves, and when they become pregnant, the unborn baby literally competes with his or her mother for available calories and nutrients, often resulting in poor prenatal growth and prematurity (5–9). This is particularly true of girls who begin menstruating early (before age twelve) and who conceive within three years after first getting their periods. Girls who begin menstruating later (after age fourteen) have finished more of their own growth (including growth of the pelvis), and if they do become pregnant, they have a lower risk of poor prenatal growth, prematurity, or complications during birth (10,11). For these reasons, nutrition during pregnancy, and particularly the pattern and amount of weight gain, have been proven to be especially important for pregnant adolescent girls (6,12–13). Females' bodies grow much more rapidly between the ages of twelve and seventeen compared to between eighteen and thirty-four. Among this younger age group, height increases by more than 3 inches, body weight by nearly 29 pounds, and body fat (as measured at the triceps, the upper arm) by 6.5 millimeters. Women in the older age group don't grow any taller; they gain only about 6 pounds in weight and 3 millimeters in body fat. From a biologic standpoint, women over the age of eighteen are better prepared physically to become pregnant, and are more likely to have healthy babies born at term.

In addition to the biologic concerns of adolescent pregnancy are the financial, social, and emotional issues, including the decision to seek prenatal care. Research shows that more than one-third of all pregnancies are unintended, including more than two-thirds among women under age twenty-five, compared to about one-fourth among women ages thirty-five to forty-four (14). In part because nearly all pregnancies to adolescent girls are unplanned, pregnant girls are much more likely to delay getting prenatal care or to receive none at all. Nearly four times as many women under the age of twenty receive late or no prenatal care compared to women aged thirty or older. The less prenatal care you receive, the greater the risks to your unborn child because the earlier you get prenatal care, the sooner any problems can be detected and treated.

Too Old?

If you are age thirty or older and pregnant, you are part of a growing trend in the United States toward delaying childbirth, a trend that started more than twenty years ago. With the availability of inexpensive and effective methods of birth control, more and more women are postponing childbearing to accommodate career choices, educational opportunities, late or second marriages, and financial considerations. In 1992 more than half of all women of reproductive age in the United States were thirty years of age or older, including one-third who were between the ages of thirty-five and forty-four. Between 1970 and 1992, among women ages thirty and older, the proportion of all births nearly doubled (from 18 percent to 32 percent), and among women ages thirty-five and older, it increased by two-thirds (from 6 percent to 10 percent)(15,16). During this same period, the proportions of first births to women ages thirty and older and ages thirty-five and older both increased fivefold (from 4 percent to 20 percent and from 1 percent to 5 percent, respectively) (15, 16).

While the trend in the 1990s may be toward delaying childbirth, it's not without drawbacks. Women over age thirty, particularly those over age thirty-five, generally have more trouble becoming pregnant and keeping the pregnancy compared to their younger counterparts (17). The encouraging news is that current research indicates that your risk of premature birth, if you are over age thirty, is less than previously believed, espe-

cially if you are in good health and have access to prenatal care.

If you're over age thirty and pregnant, it can be both
a plus and a minus. On the plus side, older mothers
tend to take better care of themselves during pregnancy; generally they register for prenatal care earlier,
have better support systems, and enjoy more economic
stability. In addition, a greater proportion of older
women are better educated, a factor shown to be associated with having healthier babies (18). For example,
between 1970 and 1992, the proportion of new mothers in their thirties who were college graduates increased from one-fourth to more than one-third,
including more than one-half of first-time mothers
(15,16). If you are one of these women, you are more
likely to seek prenatal care early, be better nourished
and gain adequate weight during pregnancy, as well as
curtail behaviors such as smoking and drinking, which
could adversely affect your pregnancy (18,19).

On the minus side, if you are age thirty or older, you
are more likely to have preexisting medical conditions
such as heart disease, diabetes, or hypertension (high
blood pressure), all of which can potentially increase
your risk of premature birth (17). Chromosomal abnormalities such as Down's syndrome are also more
common among older mothers (see Table 2). If you are
over age thirty and this is not your first pregnancy, you
are more likely to have had previous preterm births,
abortions, or other obstetrical or gynecological factors
that could increase your risk of prematurity in this
pregnancy (more about this later). Some studies have
shown that the risk of preterm birth and low birthweight is higher among women ages thirty and older,

while other studies have not (20–27). With early prenatal care, control of preexisting medical problems, and reduction of such factors as smoking and stress, you can substantially reduce much of the increased risk of preterm birth associated with being older.

Table 2.

Incidence of Down's Syndrome
Per 100,000 Live Births by Maternal Age,
United States, 1990*

All Ages	Under 20	20–24	25–29	30–34	35–39	40–49
54.4	36.7	37.7	39.9	63.0	123.3	421.2

* Data from the National Center for Health Statistics. Advance report of maternal and health data from the birth certificate, 1990. *Monthly Vital Statistics Report;* Vol. 42, No. Suppl. Hyattsville, Maryland: Public Health Service, 1993.

What's Your Household Income?

As another nonmodifiable factor (unless you win the lottery this Saturday!), your household income also influences your risk of prematurity. Women with a low income are at increased risk, although high income is no guarantee against prematurity. If you have a lower income, you may have less access to adequate prenatal care, less money for a proper prenatal diet, and other concerns. You may also lead a more stressful life. All of these factors and more may explain why low income is a risk factor for prematurity.

Are You a Single Parent?

Whether you become a single parent with this pregnancy or whether you already have other children at home, you are at an increased risk for prematurity. As a single parent (especially if you're not getting any help from family or friends) you alone shoulder the physical, emotional, and financial responsibilities of raising your children. These stresses add to your risk.

How Big Is Your Household?

Your household composition is also an important influence on your risk of prematurity because of the amount of physical effort involved in your daily life. If you have preschoolers or more than two children at home, or if an elderly relative lives with you, particularly if he or she is bedridden, wheelchair-bound, or otherwise incapacitated, your risk of prematurity is also increased because of the amount of physical effort involved in your daily life. Think of the energy you spend lifting, chasing, changing, and playing with a toddler every day. Although the numbers and ages of household members are nonmodifiable risk factors, the physical factors associated with your family and home environment *are* modifiable, and will be discussed in Chapter 4.

Gynecological, Obstetrical, and Medical Factors Present Before This Pregnancy

The second half of this chapter discusses your gynecological, obstetrical, and medical risk factors. Each time you become pregnant, you bring a unique set of risk factors to that pregnancy, different from those you might have had the last time you were pregnant. With each pregnancy you are older, which, as discussed earlier, can add to your risk. Other problems, such as medical conditions, may develop or increase as you age. If you have postponed having children, any prior spontaneous abortions and induced abortions (particularly if done in the second trimester) may also add to your risk of prematurity in this pregnancy. Gynecological and obstetrical factors present before this pregnancy may have an important influence on your current pregnancy. It is essential that you try to recall in detail past conceptions and their outcomes. These "historical" risk factors are, of course, nonmodifiable, but it is important that you identify them, since each one may add to your overall risk of prematurity. First, let's go over your gynecological, obstetrical, and medical history, then we will cover factors in your current pregnancy.

Have You Been Pregnant Before?

If one or more of your prior pregnancies ended before 24 weeks' gestation, whether spontaneously (often called a miscarriage) or induced (an abortion), your risk of prematurity in this pregnancy may be increased (28–32). Spontaneous abortions are fairly common, occurring in about one out of every five pregnancies; about one out of one hundred women experiences three or more spontaneous abortions before their first successful birth. If you have had only one prior spontaneous abortion, your risk of prematurity in this pregnancy is increased about 20 to 30 percent; with two or more prior spontaneous abortions, your risk increases to about 50 to 90 percent (28,29). How many weeks along you were when you lost the pregnancy may also be an important consideration in evaluating your risk. One recent study showed that when the loss occurred between 13 and 18 weeks' gestation, the risk of prematurity in the subsequent pregnancy was increased by about 70 percent, but if it occurred between 19 and 22 weeks, the risk was increased more than 400 percent (32).

If you have had an induced abortion before this pregnancy, you are not alone. About one out of six women in the United States has had at least one induced abortion; one out of twenty women has had two or more. Both the number of prior induced abortions and how many weeks pregnant you were when they were performed affects your current risk of prematurity (28,33–35). If you have had one or more induced abortions, your risk of prematurity with this pregnancy increases about 30 percent. If they were done during the second trimester, after 14 weeks, your subsequent risk of prematurity is greater than if they had been done during the first trimester, before 14 weeks. This difference is primarily due to the techniques used to perform induced abortion in the first versus second trimesters. The procedures for first-trimester abortion involve dilating the cervix slightly and suctioning the

Figure 3

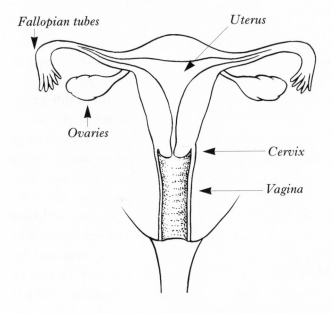

Female reproductive tract.

contents of the uterus (see Figure 3). The procedures for second-trimester abortions are more involved, including dilating the cervix wider and for longer periods, and scraping the inside of the uterus. Women who have had several second-trimester abortions may have a higher incidence of *incompetent* cervix, a premature spontaneous dilation of the cervix, because the cervix has been artificially dilated several times before this pregnancy.

Have You Given Birth Prematurely Before?

You are very likely to give birth to an infant whose gestational age and birthweight are similar to those in your earlier pregnancies (36). For this reason, if you have had a prior premature birth, especially if that infant was also low birthweight (less than 5 pounds 8 ounces), your risk of prematurity is greatly increased for this pregnancy. Overall, you are about two to three times as likely to have a child of similar gestational age and birthweight in your second pregnancy. If your first birth was premature, the risk that your second pregnancy will also be premature is increased more than threefold. If you've had two prior premature births, the risk for your third pregnancy is increased nearly sevenfold. Likewise, if your first baby was small-for-gestational age (SGA, below the 10th percentile for gestational age; see Chapter 1), or large-for-gestational age (LGA, above the 90th percentile for gestational age), you have a threefold chance of having a baby with a similar birthweight in your second pregnancy. Women who have had a prior preterm birth or SGA infant are four times more likely to deliver before 32 weeks' gestation, and nearly three times more likely to deliver before 37 weeks' gestation. Conversely, women who have had an LGA infant are about half as likely to deliver preterm. You can understand now how important it is to prevent prematurity, not only for this pregnancy, but for your future pregnancies as well.

Is This Your First or Your Fifth Pregnancy?

The number of times you have given birth before this pregnancy is also an important consideration in assessing your total risk. Scientists are not completely clear why, but if this is your first pregnancy or if you have given birth four or more times before, you are at an increased risk for prematurity. If any infant from a previous pregnancy was low birthweight (weighed less than 5 pounds 8 ounces), a stillborn (born dead), or died during the first month after birth (neonatal death), these all add to your risk in this pregnancy.

Is This Pregnancy the Result of Infertility Treatments?

If you have had infertility treatments and are now pregnant, congratulations! You've already gone through a difficult process successfully. Unfortunately, having had infertility treatment is a risk factor for prematurity. About one out of ten women in the United States has difficulty becoming pregnant, and about half seek infertility treatments. Based on data from a national study of infertility, about two out of five women and their partners undergo tests, about one out of five women receive ovulation-inducing medications, about one out of ten women undergo treatment for blocked Fallopian tubes, and about one out of fifty women receive in vitro fertilization (37). Pregnancies that result from infertility treatment, particularly in vitro fertilization, may be at high risk for prematurity. A recent international survey of pregnancy outcomes after in vitro fertilization reported a 10 to 20 percent incidence of premature births, depending on whether there had been a previous induced abortion (38). Other studies have reported a 2-fold higher risk of preterm birth after a history of infertility (33).

Did Your Mother Take DES When She Was Pregnant with You?

Between the late 1940s and early 1970s, the drug diethylstilbestrol (DES) was frequently prescribed to prevent spontaneous abortions. An estimated 1 million to 1.5 million daughters of women who took this drug are now of reproductive age and are at an increased risk themselves of delivering their own babies prematurely. Women who were exposed to this drug before they themselves were born have higher incidences of infertility, as well as spontaneous abortions, ectopic pregnancies, and premature births (39,40). The risk of premature birth is greatest among women who were exposed to this drug before birth and who experienced malformations of the uterus, cervix, or vagina. Find out from your mother if she took this medication when she was pregnant with you. If she can't remember or is not sure, her doctor may still have her records or it may be in your pediatrician's records. It's worth the effort to find out, since research has shown this to be a strong risk factor for prematurity.

Do You Have Any Medical Problems?

Medical conditions, even if they are well controlled, add to your overall risk of prematurity. As mentioned earlier, age is a risk factor for prematurity because the incidences of many medical conditions—such as diabetes, chronic hypertension (high blood pressure), and heart disease—increase with age. For example, among all women giving birth in the United States, the incidences of heart disease, diabetes, and chronic hypertension were 1.7 times higher, 2.6 times higher, and 3.3 times higher, respectively, for women ages thirty and older compared to women under age thirty. All three of these medical conditions can cause changes in the structure of blood vessels, and are therefore associated with higher incidences of both poor fetal growth and prematurity.

Factors in Your Current Pregnancy

Now that we have covered your "historical" risk factors, let's move on to what's happening right now in your current pregnancy. The factors I'm going to discuss are also nonmodifiable, but are important to include in your overall risk assessment.

Have You Had Any Bleeding?

When the embryo implants in the lining of the uterus, you may experience a slight amount of bleeding (usually near the time of your first missed menstrual period). But bleeding at any time thereafter is a warning sign that something is wrong. Call your doctor right away! If the embryo has not implanted well, or has implanted in a poor location within the uterus, the pregnancy will most likely be lost very early, sometimes even before you realize you're pregnant. If the embryo has implanted near the opening of the uterus (the cervix), it is likely that there will be bleeding as the placenta grows. Depending on the exact location, such placental complications are associated with an in-

Call Your Doctor Immediately If You Experience Any of the Following Symptoms:

1. Loss of blood or watery fluid from the vagina
2. Sudden swelling of your face or fingers
3. Severe headache
4. Changes in your vision, such as blurring or dimness
5. Menstrual-like cramps or pain in your abdomen
6. Persistent vomiting, chills, or fever

Information to Have at Hand When You Speak with Your Doctor:

1. If you are bleeding, be prepared to give your doctor (or the nurse answering the call) details, such as amount, when it started, if there is any pain and where, and if you are also experiencing cramps.

2. For the other symptoms, be able to give information about when they started, severity (i.e., how high is your fever, and when did you last take your temperature), and any associated events (i.e., you had taken a fall an hour earlier, one of your other children came home sick from school yesterday).

3. Have at least four telephone numbers at hand, including two neighbors (one might be out when you call), your husband or partner, and the pharmacy. Depending on what your doctor advises, whether to come to his or her office or the hospital as soon as possible, or to call in a prescription, you will be prepared.

creased risk of prematurity, as well as being an emergency situation for both mother and infant (see Figures 4a and 4b). About one out of ten births before 32 weeks' gestation are complicated by bleeding, compared to about one out of twenty births before 37

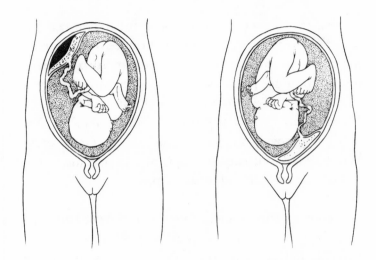

Placental complications. **Figure 4A** *(left)*: *abruptio placentae.* **Figure 4B** *(right)*: *placenta previa.*

weeks and one out of fifty births after 37 weeks. Placenta previa occurs when the placenta covers all or part of the cervix, detaching as the cervix dilates, or opens, during labor. If the placenta detaches from the uterus before or during labor (a condition known as abruptio placentae), the oxygen supply to the unborn baby is suddenly decreased and the baby must be delivered immediately. As in medical conditions, the incidence of bleeding during pregnancy after the first trimester also parallels increasing maternal age: Bleeding during pregnancy is about 50 percent higher among women ages thirty and older compared to their younger counterparts.

Another complication associated with a much higher risk of preterm birth is incompetent cervix, which was mentioned earlier when I discussed induced abortions. This complication occurs when the mouth of the uterus, the cervix, dilates before full-term gestation. The term *incompetent* means that the cervix doesn't remain closed until labor begins, as it should. Instead, it begins to open, painlessly, weeks or months before the normal end of pregnancy (see Figures 5A and 5B). Many women who have lost several pregnancies are finally diagnosed as having an incompetent cervix. When diagnosed early enough, the cervix may be sutured to keep it closed until term, when the stitches are cut.

A complication related to incompetent cervix is premature rupture of the membranes, abbreviated as PROM. Before birth, the unborn baby is floating in a sac filled with amniotic fluid. When this sac (also called fetal membranes) ruptures before the pregnancy has reached term, the risk of premature birth is greatly increased: one out of five births before 32 weeks' gestation had PROM compared to one out of eight births before 37 weeks and one out of twenty-five after 37 weeks. PROM can also occur in the absence of an incompetent cervix. One recent national study reported three factors that are each significantly associated with PROM: bleeding in more than one trimester, prior preterm birth, and cigarette smoking in the current pregnancy (41). Birth before 32 weeks is ten times more likely with the diagnosis of incompetent cervix and five times more likely with uterine bleeding or PROM.

Have You Experienced Any Discharge or Itching?

Although prior vaginal infections may have affected your ability to become pregnant, perhaps by causing

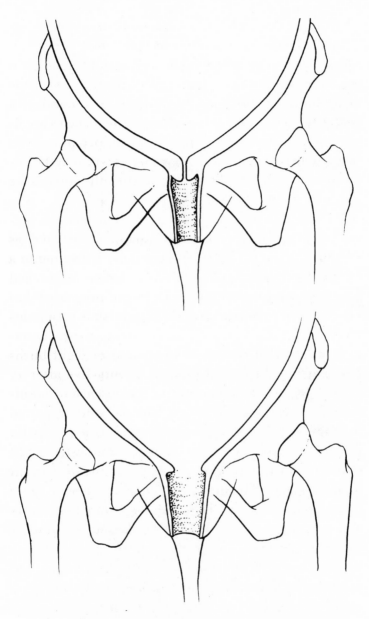

Figure 5A (top): *normal, closed cervix.* *Figure 5B* (bottom): *incompetent cervix.*

scarring of the Fallopian tubes, they have little influence on your current pregnancy. However, if you experience symptoms of a vaginal infection while you are pregnant, such as pain and itching, unusual discharge or a foul smell, tell your health-care provider so the problem can be diagnosed and treated promptly. Untreated vaginal infections can result in a premature birth, with or without accompanying PROM (42).

Are You Pregnant with Multiples?

If you are, you have lots of company! In 1992 in the United States, there were nearly 100,000 multiple births, including more than 95,000 twin births and nearly 3,900 triplet and higher order births (including quadruplets, quintuplets) (16). More than half of all singleton births were to women between the ages of twenty and twenty-nine, whereas more than half of all twin births and two-thirds of all triplet and higher order births were to women ages twenty-five to thirty-four (43). Preterm birth is five times more likely in twin births and nearly nine times more likely in triplet and higher order births. As a result, low birthweight (less than 5 pounds 8 ounces) is ten times more common among twin infants and nearly twenty times more common among infants of triplet and higher order births (44). Reducing modifiable risk factors are therefore particularly important if you are pregnant with multiples. Nutrition is one of the few factors that has been shown to improve the growth of multiples before birth (more about this in Chapter 6). Other nutritional factors have also been shown to be associated with prematurity, such as low maternal weight gain before 20 weeks' gestation and iron-deficiency anemia (low blood iron); these will also be discussed in detail in Chapter 6.

These "traditional" risk factors, as summarized in the following Checklist 1, are the ones most health-care providers ask about. Recognizing these factors is a good start, but obviously it's not enough, since prematurity has been steadily rising, even among women without these traditional risk factors. The majority of the risk factors I'm going to talk about for the remainder of this book center on this critical advice: Since premature contractions are very difficult to stop once they've started, the best way to prevent prematurity is to prevent premature contractions. Most of the factors I'm going to discuss lead, either directly or indirectly, to premature contractions, and therefore premature birth. It's important for you to understand the physical basis of the relationship between standing, stress, and other factors and premature contractions; this is the topic for the next chapter.

Checklist 1. Traditional Risk Factors

FAMILY BACKGROUND	Nonmodifiable	Modifiable	Modified
Race and ethnicity			
U.S.-born vs. foreign-born			
Age <18 or >35 (>30 if 1st birth)			
Low family income			
Single parent			
Preschool children at home			
More than two children at home			
Elderly relative at home			
GYN, OB, AND MEDICAL	*Nonmodifiable*	*Modifiable*	*Modified*
Historic			
Prior spontaneous abortions			
Prior induced abortions			
Prior preterm birth			
Prior low-birthweight infant			
No prior births			
Four or more prior births			
Prior stillbirth			
Prior neonatal death			
History of infertility			
History of DES exposure			
Preexisting medical problems			

44

GYN, OB, AND MEDICAL *(cont.)*	Nonmodifiable	Modifiable	Modified
Current			
Bleeding after the first trimester			
Placental complications			
Incompetent cervix			
Premature rupture of membranes (PROM)			
Infection			
Multiple gestation			

45

3

The Physiology of Preterm Labor: What's Going On in Your Body?

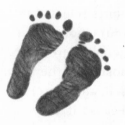

"My contractions started when I was arguing with my mother on the phone. I don't even remember what the argument was about. All I remember was this feeling like a knot in my belly tightening and loosening every few minutes. At first I ignored it, but the more we shouted at each other, the stronger the feelings became. When I finally hung up the phone, I realized I was having premature contractions and I panicked. I called my doctor and he told me to get to the hospital. The doctors examined me to see if I had broken my bag of waters, put me on a monitor to time the contractions, and gave me fluid and medications by IV to try to stop my labor. The medications didn't work because the contractions continued and within about twelve hours my bag of waters did break. My labor continued, and by the next day I had given birth. I guess I was fortunate because I was only about a month premature, and my daughter was big for her age, about 6 pounds 6 ounces. To this day, though, my mother feels guilty for making me go into premature labor."

Do you think arguing with her mother caused this woman to have preterm contractions? I do, at least in part. Premature contractions can be caused by many factors, some of them mechanical, such as standing, while others are chemical, such as the hormones released under stress or anger. Once premature contractions begin, they are very difficult to stop. Although there are medications that can be tried, for the most part they work poorly or not at all. Your best plan, therefore, is to prevent premature contractions, because if they cannot be stopped they lead to labor and premature birth. In this chapter I am going to discuss how stress, standing, and other factors can lead to premature contractions, how to recognize premature contractions, and what to do if they occur.

The Physics of Pregnancy

Before you became pregnant, your uterus was nestled deep in your pelvis, so far down that you probably couldn't feel it if you tried. Your pelvis also cradled your ovaries, which are located on each side of the uterus. The uterus is an amazing muscular organ, growing from about $2\frac{1}{2}$ ounces in weight and capable of holding only about $\frac{1}{3}$ ounce of fluid before pregnancy to about 3½ ounces in weight and capable of holding about 64 ounces or more (a half gallon!) at term! As the pregnant uterus grows, it expands up and out of the pelvis (see Figure 6A). By about 12 weeks' gestation, the uterus has cleared the pubic bone and you can feel it fairly easily. Between 14 and 18 weeks, the uterus will have reached about halfway between your pubic bone and your umbilicus (your belly button). By 20 to 22 weeks, the uterus will have reached your umbilicus or be even a little above it. By 28 weeks, the uterus has reached halfway between your umbilicus and sternum (breastbone). At term, 40 weeks, the uterus has reached your sternum, or the point at the top of your ribcage. No wonder you've got heartburn! When your doctor stretches a tape measure from your pubic bone up over your expanding belly, he or she is measuring the expansion of your uterus.

The Effects of Standing

The uterus has an enormous blood supply, and these arteries and veins become enlarged as your pregnancy progresses, supplying the placenta, uterus, and growing baby with oxygen and nutrients, and carrying away toxins and waste products. The lining of the uterus is itself a rich capillary bed that supports the placenta and baby. On the outside of the uterus is a dense network of arteries and veins. As the uterus grows and expands to fill the pelvis, it enlarges in both width and height. The arteries and veins along the outside of the pelvis are compressed between the expanding uterus, which is fairly solid because it's filled with amniotic

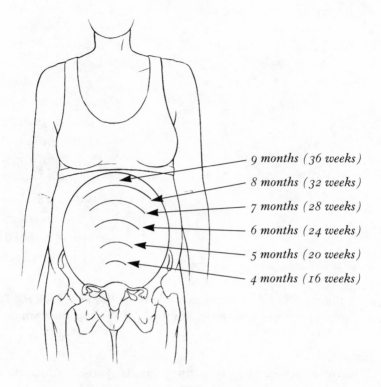

9 months (36 weeks)
8 months (32 weeks)
7 months (28 weeks)
6 months (24 weeks)
5 months (20 weeks)
4 months (16 weeks)

Size and location of uterus by monthly gestation.

fluid, and the bony pelvis, which supports the growing uterus. This compression increases after 12 weeks' gestation, when the uterus has grown beyond the rim of the pelvis (see Figure 6A). When you stand for any length of time after 12 weeks' gestation, this compression becomes even worse, and as a result, blood has difficulty returning from the lower part of your body back to your heart. Unless you sit down, or better yet, lie down, this congestion can cause your uterus to begin to contract in an attempt to change its shape and relieve the blockage (1–5) (see Figures 6B and 6C). This is

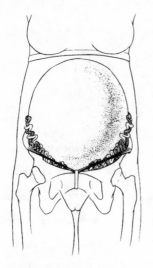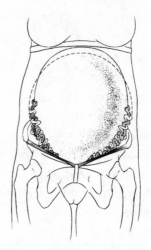

Figure 6B *(left): compression of arteries and veins between the uterus and bony pelvis.* **Figure 6B** *(right): how this compression is relieved when the uterus begins to contract.*

termed the vena cava syndrome. If you continue to stand, your uterus will contract even more regularly, and preterm labor may begin.

With regular contractions, the cervix—the gateway between the uterus and vagina—begins to thin out (efface) and open (dilate). When the cervix has opened enough, the amniotic sac breaks, and it becomes much more difficult to stop labor, as well as prevent infection. Regular contractions are what leads to premature labor. Painless, irregular contractions, which you may or may not be aware of, occur naturally throughout pregnancy; these are called Braxton-Hicks contractions and are perfectly normal.

Standing for long periods can also reduce your unborn baby's ultimate birthweight. When the blood supply is blocked, both the placenta and the baby do not receive as much oxygen and nutrients as they should. The result may be lower birthweight, as well as the presence of placental infarcts, areas where the placental tissue died due to lack of oxygen. Data from the Collaborative Perinatal Project, a study of nearly 56,000 women, showed that placental infarcts increased with standing (6). Compared to nonemployed mothers, employed mothers with sedentary jobs, and employed mothers who quit work before 33 weeks' gestation, the frequency of placental infarcts was twice as great among mothers who quit work between 33 and 37 weeks' gestation, and five times as great among mothers who continued to work after 37 weeks' gestation. The American Medical Association recommends that during pregnancy you stand for no more than four hours at a time after 24 weeks' gestation, and no more than thirty minutes in an hour after 32 weeks' gestation (7).

The Effects of Lifting and Carrying

Take a deep breath and tighten your stomach muscles. This is what you automatically do when you lift something, especially if it's heavy or awkward. When you take a deep breath and tighten your stomach muscles, you're actually forcing down on your abdomen and uterus as well. This increase in pressure is another factor that can lead to premature contractions. For this reason, you should avoid lifting and carrying as much as possible during pregnancy. Some lifting and carrying is unavoidable—especially if you have small chil-

Figure 7A

Lifting improperly increases pressure on the uterus.

dren—but make a conscious effort to reduce it as much as possible. How often and how much you lift are also important considerations: Repetitive lifting is worse than intermittent, and heavy lifting is worse than light. The American Medical Association recommends that pregnant women should not do repetitive lifting of more than 50 pounds beyond 20 weeks' gestation, and no more than 24 to 50 pounds beyond 24 weeks' gestation (7). They also recommend that pregnant women do no intermittent lifting of more than 50 pounds beyond 30 weeks' gestation. These are general recommendations; your obstetrician may want to modify

Lifting properly, with your legs, reduces pressure on the uterus.

them further for your individual situation—talk it over with him or her.

If you must lift something, try to use proper body mechanics to minimize the stress (see Figures 7A and 7B). Bend at the knees instead of reaching down to lift. Hold the object close to your body; not at arm's length. And when you straighten up, use your legs, not your back.

The Effects of Stress

You know that feeling you get just before you have to give a speech? Or when your dentist says, "Open wide"? Or when you're deep in thought and suddenly a door slams? Or when you're walking across the street and are almost hit by a turning car? Or when you're waiting for a parking spot and someone else slips in before you? All of these feelings are triggered by hormones that make our hearts race and our blood pressures soar, giving a surge of energy we never knew we had. Often called a "flight or fight" response, the hormonal reaction to *acute stress* temporarily gives us greater physical and emotional abilities, so we can hop out of the way of that turning car or muster the courage to give a speech.

We all experience both acute and chronic physical and mental stress in our daily lives. Imagine trying to cook dinner and the phone starts to ring, the pots are boiling over, the dog is barking, and the baby is crying (because he can sense all this tension!). If you were in this situation, would you say you were cool and collected, even-tempered and efficient? Not unless you were Secret Agent 007, who was always cool and calm under any kind of situation! No, you would probably be getting a headache (your blood pressure was rising) and become short-tempered, irritable, and disorganized. Chronic stress includes situations or events that happen every day or periodically, like traffic jams every morning during your commute to work, having to wait on lines every time you go grocery shopping, or having to listen to a neighbor's dog barking for hours every evening.

Driving can also be a source of stress, particularly during pregnancy. Traffic jams, thoughtless or rude drivers, road construction, bad weather, backseat drivers, and noisy children can all add up to stress while driving, and during pregnancy that stress can lead to premature contractions! Try to limit the amount of driving you do while pregnant, especially during the second half of your pregnancy, when it may be frustrating just fitting behind the wheel!

When you're under stress, you might even get a stomachache or cramps. Even the uterus responds to stress, by cramping. Both physical and mental stress result in an increased production of the catecholamine hormones norepinephrine and epinephrine. Norepinephrine increases during heavy physical activity, exposure to cold, and aggressive reactions; epinephrine increases with mental or emotional stress, such as noise, pain or discomfort, anxiety, or apprehension. Together they increase your blood pressure and heart rate, shunt blood away from your uterus and stomach, and increase your metabolism. Digestion shuts down, but the production of acid continues to increase under stress. When the stress hormone levels went down, your uterus and stomach received their regular blood supply once more and you became conscious of hunger pangs. That explains why you were so hungry after giving that speech, having that argument, or coming home from the dentist!

Physical exertion also causes a release of catecholamines, increasing the risk of prematurity. By physical exertion I mean climbing stairs and ladders, stooping and bending below knee level, and any other activity that involves the large muscles of the arms, back, and legs. Such physical exertion also draws blood away from the uterus to the muscles that are being used, decreasing the flow of oxygen and nutrients to the uterus, the placenta, and the baby. In addition, physical activity increases caloric requirements, and your needs are met at the expense of your unborn baby. For these reasons, women who do engage in substantial physical exertion throughout their pregnancies tend to have much smaller infants at higher risk of being premature. The American Medical Association recommends that pregnant women not climb ladders or poles more than four times in eight hours beyond 20 weeks' gestation and not climb stairs more than four times in eight hours beyond 28 weeks' gestation (7). They also recommend that pregnant women refrain from repetitive stooping and bending more than ten times per hour beyond 20 weeks' gestation, or two to ten times per hour beyond 28 weeks' gestation (7).

Studies with animals have shown that an increase in catecholamines in the mother's circulation results in an increase in blood pressure, constriction of the uterine blood vessels, and a reduction in the amount of oxygen received by the fetus (8,9). Preeclampsia, a complication of pregnancy caused by high blood pressure, is also associated with an increase in maternal catecholamines (10). Recent studies with pregnant women have shown a strong association between stress and preterm birth and low birthweight (less than 5½ pounds) (11–14). The chronic stress of major life events—serious illnesses; financial, domestic, or legal problems for a pregnant woman; or the problems of close friends or family—has also been linked to an increase in both preterm and low birthweight (13,14).

Identifying and Reducing Stress

Potentially everything in our lives can contribute to our total stress. Many unavoidable major life crises cause stress, such as financial problems, death in the family, being fired from work. Even positive events—like getting married, becoming pregnant, or graduating from school—add stress to our lives. Health is a reflection of our bodies' abilities to balance all our physical and mental processes. Change, whether positive or negative, challenges our bodies to adapt. Too much change can drain our adaptive abilities, causing physical and mental symptoms of stress. Two American doctors, T. H. Holmes and R. H. Rahe, have devised the Social Readjustment Ratings Scale (see Table 3), which quantifies the stress in our lives over a one-year period. As you can see from the scale, even so-called happy events such as vacation and Christmas add stress to our lives. Take a minute to add up your own stresses from the Holmes Rahe Scale. If you scored more than 300 points, your risk of experiencing stress-related illness is greatly increased; if your score was between 150 and 299, it is increased moderately; and if your score was less than 150, your risk is increased only mildly.

We each experience stress in different ways, and a situation which is stressful to one person may actually be pleasurable to another. Stress signals include nervous reflexes (e.g., biting nails, grinding teeth, twirling

Table 3. The Holmes Rahe Scale

Life Event	Life Change Units
Death of a spouse	100
Divorce	73
Marital separation	65
Imprisonment	63
Death of a close family member	63
Personal injury or illness	53
Marriage	50
Dismissal from work	47
Marital reconciliation	45
Retirement	45
Change in health of a family member	44
Pregnancy	40
Sexual difficulties	39
Gain of a new family member	39
Business readjustment	39
Change in financial state	38
Change in number of arguments with spouse	35
Major mortgage	32
Foreclosure of mortgage or loan	30
Change in responsibilities at work	29
Son or daughter leaving home	29
Trouble with in-laws	29
Outstanding personal achievement	28
Spouse begins or stops work	26
Begin or end school	26
Change in living conditions	25
Revision of personal habits	24
Trouble with boss	23
Change in work hours or conditions	20
Change in residence	20
Change in schools	20
Change in recreation	19
Change in church activities	19
Change in social activities	18
Minor mortgage or loan	17
Change in sleeping habits	16
Change in number of family reunions	15
Change in eating habits	15
Vacation	13
Christmas	12
Minor violation of the law	11

hair), mood changes (e.g., depression, hostility, impatience, anxiety), behavior changes (e.g., overreacting, insomnia, emotional outbreaks), and stress-related illnesses (e.g., migraine headaches, digestive disorders, skin outbreaks, sexual problems). During pregnancy these problems may become even worse because you are also coping with changes in your body image, family structure, roles for you and your partner, personal space at home, and financial responsibilities. All the more reason to take a good hard look at yourself and your life to assess your stresses, how you cope with them, and make positive changes.

Because you cannot always eliminate the acute and chronic stresses in your life, try to cope with them better. Some of the most successful stress-reducing methods have been Lamaze techniques, those used during childbirth, when you are trying to handle pain that can last over many hours. One of the first things you will be taught if you attend Lamaze classes is how to breathe—slow and deep, with cleansing breaths—which, in turn, will keep your heart rate down and give you a better sense of control and well-being. Next, you will learn to focus—during childbirth, on your contractions, but in everyday life, on whatever stress you are dealing with. By calmly focusing your attention on the job at hand, whether it's navigating an icy stretch of road with a carful of noisy toddlers, or rushing to meet a deadline before the last mail collection, you *can* learn to reduce the amount of stress you experience. Try several techniques to figure out which best fits you and your situation. Whether or not you are pregnant, stress-reduction techniques can help you deal with the frustrations of daily living in a more efficient and healthful manner. For recommended reading in this area, see the Bibliography at the end of this book.

The following are five proven techniques for reducing stress in your daily life, and are useful both during and after pregnancy:

Time Management: As will be discussed in Chapter 4, becoming more organized, streamlining and simplifying tasks at home and work, delegating responsibilities, and setting priorities can reduce stress.

Nutrition: As will be discussed in Chapters 5 and 6, a well-balanced diet benefits not only you and your unborn baby, but also helps you cope more effectively with life's stresses. Drinking too much coffee and using alcohol and cigarettes to relieve stress is not only unhealthy for you and your baby, but can cause nutritional imbalances, mood and behavior changes, and actually increase the amount of stress you experience and decrease your ability to cope effectively.

Exercise: Also discussed in Chapter 5, exercise can help your physical and mental well-being, including improving your digestion and sleep habits. During pregnancy, though, the type and intensity of exercise are important factors in your overall risk of prematurity. An ideal exercise during pregnancy is yoga, which is particularly recommended if you have a lot of stress in your life and should not participate in strenuous physical activity. Yoga improves your flexibility and body tone (see Figure 8). Obviously, more strenuous activities don't mix with pregnancy; ask your doctor which gentle exercise suits you best.

Figure 8

The lotus position.

Meditation: This technique reduces stress by emptying the conscious mind. A technique that has been practiced for over 2,500 years, it is the simplest method, practiced alone wherever you can find a quiet space. Based on the physiological connection between mind and body, successful meditation results in a reduction of tension and physical stress, a clearer, more focused mind, and a calmer overall sense of being.

Massage: This technique eases away muscular tension and results in a more relaxed body and calmer outlook. It also gives you a set amount of quiet time in which you clear your mind and totally relax. For many busy people with hectic schedules, a weekly massage is the most important investment they can make for their mental and physical well-being.

Recognizing Premature Contractions

If you have already given birth before this pregnancy, you can more easily recognize the sensation of uterine contractions, although they will be much less intense than what you experienced during any previous labor. If you have never given birth, appreciating the sensation of a uterine contraction is more difficult. In addition, not all women feel contractions in the same way—ask any two women about their labor experience, and you will probably hear two completely different stories. For one woman, the contractions she felt before and during labor may have been very intense and severe. For another woman, contractions may have been moderate or mild, no worse than monthly menstrual cramps. Or for medical reasons, she may have undergone a cesarean section (surgical birth) before she went into labor, never feeling any contractions at all. So keep in mind that uterine contractions may or may not be painful: Every woman is different, and even for the same woman, each pregnancy is different.

When your body goes into normal, full-term labor, beginning contractions are generally milder, spaced far apart, short, and somewhat irregular. (You time contractions from the beginning of one contraction to the beginning of the next one.) As labor proceeds, contractions become stronger, closer together, and more regular. The closer together and the stronger they are, the harder they are to stop.

Uterine contractions are usually perceived as a heaviness in the abdomen or as pain in the mid- to lower back, accompanied by a tightening of the uterus. Some women say the tightness feels like a fist squeezing inside their belly. When you feel this heaviness or pain, you should place your hands on your abdomen, at the top of your uterus, to determine if these sensations are accompanied by a tightening or hardening of your uterus (see Figure 9). When you squeeze your biceps to "make a muscle" in your arm, you can feel the muscle then go from elastic to hard. When your uterus contracts, you can feel the tightening the same way.

After you detect uterine contractions, you should determine what you were doing when they occurred. As discussed earlier, the activities that cause uterine contractions vary greatly from woman to woman. For example, for one woman it may be standing on the train during her commute home, carrying groceries, or hanging wallpaper. For another woman, it may be standing for long periods while shopping, carrying a child in her arms, or vacuuming the rugs. For a third, it may be an argument with a co-worker or a stressful session of bill paying. Regardless of the activity, it is important for you to:

1. Recognize that uterine contractions are occurring;
2. Identify what activities bring on the contractions; and
3. Stop that activity and sit down, or preferably, lie down on your left side, until the contractions subside.

Figure 9

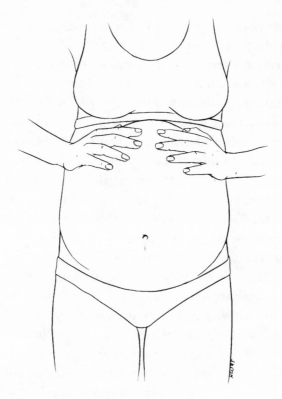

How to feel for uterine contractions.

4. Drink at least a glass or two of water, since dehydration can also cause uterine contractions.
5. Call your doctor immediately and report your contractions. Follow his or her advice.

This increased awareness of your body will enable you to prevent uterine contractions and to cope more effectively when they do occur.

Labor is preceded by one or more of the following signs: painful, recurrent uterine contractions; passage of a small amount of blood-tinged mucus (called "bloody show") a few days before labor; or a sudden gush of amniotic fluid from the vagina (rupture of the bag of waters, or membranes). True labor pains are characterized by both their intensity and duration. At the beginning of labor, the pain may be perceived as a slight backache, which then radiates to the abdomen. These early contractions may be as brief as thirty seconds, whereas later they may last for as long as two minutes. True labor pains are rhythmic even during early labor, occurring every fifteen to twenty minutes. After a few hours, the pains occur about every five minutes. False labor occurs when the painful contractions diminish in intensity after a few hours, and labor does not progress. It is often very difficult to distinguish between true labor and false labor, and since it is better to err on the side of safety, it is prudent to follow the five steps outlined above when you are feeling painful contractions. As discussed earlier (Chapter 2), if you experience a sudden gush of fluid from the vagina, with or without painful contractions, call your doctor immediately.

What to Do If You Go into Premature Labor: A Game Plan of Action

If the contractions do not subside despite these steps, it is important for you to have a "game plan of action." This plan includes the recruitment of help from several contact people, such as friends, relatives, neighbors, and co-workers. Each member of the game plan "team" should have every other member's telephone number at home and work, including car phone and pager numbers, as well as the telephone numbers of your obstetrician and the hospital where you plan to deliver. They should all know where the hospital is located and the shortest route to get there, as well as the nearest hospitals to your home and work, just in case.

When you get to the hospital, you will be admitted to the maternity unit. The nursing staff on these units are specially trained to help you and want only what's best for you and your baby. Depending on your symptoms, the nurse (or interns or residents, physicians-in-training) will listen to the baby's heartbeat, feel the baby's position by placing their hands on your abdomen, take your pulse and blood pressure, and may even perform a vaginal exam to determine if your bag of waters has ruptured. A monitor may be placed around your abdomen to track the baby's heartbeat and to record the duration and intensity of the uterine contractions. An intravenous line may also be started, both to give you fluids and to administer medications to try to stop labor. If you are in false labor or if your contractions subside completely, and your bag of waters has not ruptured, you will be allowed to return home as soon as possible. For some women, this scenario may be repeated several times before they actually give birth.

The next chapter will focus on your home and work environments, helping you identify mental and physical stresses in your daily life. It may not be possible to modify every stress or risk, but even small positive changes will add up in your favor. Remember: Preventing prematurity is really a short-term challenge, ranging from a few days or weeks to as long as six months. Each day that prematurity is prevented is another day your unborn child grows stronger and healthier!

4

Your Home and Work Environments

IN THIS CHAPTER we're going to examine your home and work environments to identify and modify risk factors for prematurity. These include both mental and physical factors, including standing, noise, physical effort (i.e., lifting and carrying), and driving. At the end of this chapter is a checklist for your use in keeping track of the risks you've identified and those you've been able to modify or eliminate.

HOW MUCH DO YOU stand during a typical day? If you are like most of us, probably quite a bit! At home we stand to wash dishes, do laundry, make dinner, put away clothes, or even just talk to family members. For those of us who work outside the home, we may stand during the commute by train, subway, or bus, while waiting for the copier to finish, running errands, and making deliveries. For many women, standing is part of their job, and they may never have thought twice about its effect on their health and the health of their unborn children. In assessing your personal risks, you need to take a closer look at things you take for granted, like standing, and make changes wherever you can. Part of reducing the amount of physical effort in your daily life centers around being more organized. People who are organized always seem to take less time and effort to do things, have more energy, and are better pre- pared. Sound like someone you'd like to be more like? Well, let me help you get more organized, more effi- cient in how you do things, and you will find that you will reduce the amount of physical effort in your daily life and improve your chances for a healthy, full-term pregnancy.

If this is not your first pregnancy, you already know that infants require an enormous amount of time and attention. If this is your first pregnancy, you'll soon learn that this one little person will monopolize your time and energies like no one you've ever known be- fore! In either case, whether this is your first child or your fifth, getting more organized can only help, both before and after the birth.

Have you ever noticed how organized people seem to have everything at their fingertips—they don't get up a dozen times from their chairs to finish something. It's a pleasure to watch a cook in an organized kitchen— everything is within arm's reach, there's not a single wasted motion, and it all seems almost effortless. Well, organized people *do* expend less physical effort because they have planned ahead. Let's go through your home and workplace and reduce the amount of physical effort you spend in your daily life. Let's start at home.

Kitchen

What are the main activities you do in your kitchen? Cook and clean up. Think about how you can become more organized and efficient in your kitchen. The first step is to clear away the clutter—from the countertops, cabinets, closets, and drawers—so your kitchen is easier to work in and easier to keep clean. Sort through and throw out what you don't need. Remember: The more objects that fill your house, the more housework (physical effort) you have to do.

The second step is to reduce the amount of standing you do while in your kitchen. Depending on the size and layout of your kitchen, you might put three- or four-legged stools (preferably one with a chair back, as in Figure 10) by the sink, stove, and one by the countertop near the telephone so that you'll be more likely to sit while washing dishes, cooking dinner, chopping vegetables, or talking to friends. When you're cooking, get out all the ingredients at once so you won't keep darting between refrigerator, cupboards, and countertops. Having a place to sit in the kitchen also increases the likelihood that you won't stand while reading recipes, writing out grocery lists, or waiting for the cookies to be done! Ask family members to take turns cooking. Order in now and then if you can afford it. If sitting isn't practical for certain kitchen chores, at least try to rest the weight of one

Figure 10

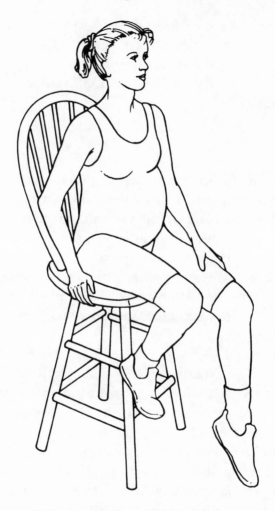

Sitting on a high stool with a chair back.

leg at a time by putting one foot on a low stepstool (see Figures 11A and 11B). This will also take some pressure off your back. A small step- or footstool is something you'll want to have after the baby comes anyway, to elevate your feet while sitting during feeding and nursing.

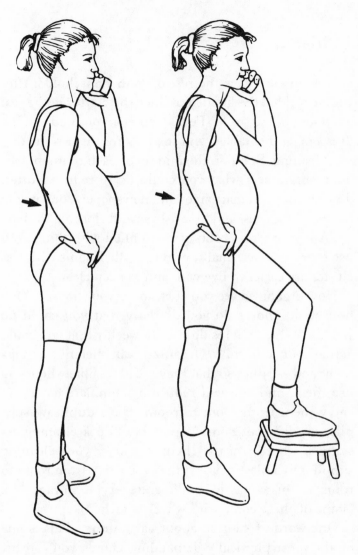

Relieving lower-back pressure by standing with a stepstool.

Cleaning

How organized is the rest of your household? After you've tackled the kitchen, reduce the clutter in the rest of your home, too. Fewer objects on end tables, dressers, coffee tables, and mantels means less dusting and cleaning. Stand in the middle of each room in your home and assess what you could do to reduce clutter: Throw away old magazines and newspapers, donate old books to libraries, and bric-a-brac and clothing to charity. Are your closets and drawers filled with things you use every day, seasonally, or not at all? Rooms with less clutter are easier to live with and to keep clean.

How organized are you at cleaning your house? What household chores do you do daily that you could do weekly? Which chores do you do weekly that you could actually do monthly? Organize your cleaning equipment and supplies so that they are accessible where you use them, and you will reduce or eliminate having to carry them from room to room. Have duplicate supplies on different floors if possible. Stock cleaning essentials where you use them. Or keep your cleaning supplies in a plastic basket that you carry from room to room or in a plastic "milk crate"–type storage box (some of these come with wheels attached).

One word of caution about vacuuming: This is one of the most physically demanding chores you can do. Cardiologists actually judge how long a nonpregnant woman can vacuum as a kind of treadmill test for endurance! If at all possible, recruit others to do the vacuuming while you are pregnant. As a matter of fact, I strongly encourage recruitment of family members and friends for all household tasks. Let others share the responsibilities and rewards of running a house—everyone will benefit.

There's another household task I strongly urge you to delegate: cleaning the cat's litter box. Not only does this chore involve a lot of lifting and bending, it could put you at risk for getting toxoplasmosis, an infection borne by cat feces that can seriously damage unborn babies. Toxoplasmosis can also be contracted by handling soil in which animals have defecated, so always wear gloves while gardening.

Laundry

Keep in mind that your objective is to reduce the amount of physical effort you exert in your home environment, including standing, carrying, lifting, and stair climbing. Two issues to consider with laundry are how you do it and how often you do it. If you have a washer and dryer in your home, it should ideally be close to the kitchen, bathrooms, and bedrooms—where most of the laundry is generated. To reduce the amount of carrying you do, have family members drop off and pick up their laundry. Better yet—teach them to do it themselves if possible. In addition, a rolling wire clothes basket is helpful for distant bedrooms or when gathering up laundry. Put a chair or three-legged stool in the laundry room to reduce the amount of standing you do while waiting to add softener to the rinse cycle or folding clean clothes. As with your cleaning supplies, have all essential laundry supplies near at hand in your laundry room to save additional steps.

Another issue to consider with laundry is how often you do it. Could you cut down doing laundry from once a week to twice a month if you bought an additional set of sheets, a few extra kitchen towels, or half a dozen new pairs of underwear? Do you wait until you have a full load of laundry or do you frequently do a load with only a few items? Keep in mind that ironing is another household activity you could do while sitting if you can't delegate it. Consider sending your shirts out to the dry cleaner if you can afford it; then you'll have one less bit of washing and ironing to do. To prevent wrinkling, remove clothes from the dryer as quickly as possible. Similarly, save time and effort ironing by first placing wrinkled clothes, such as cotton shirts and pants, in the dryer for a few minutes.

Grocery Shopping and Chores

As with laundry and cleaning, consider how often you shop and do such chores as picking up and dropping off dry cleaning. Aside from the physical effort of walking down aisles and standing at the checkout counter, for many women grocery shopping also means the stress of fighting traffic and finding parking spaces, not to mention bending to lift items out of the cart, then loading them into the car. Better yet, have someone go along with you to bend, lift, and carry.

Try to cut down on the frequency of food shopping by buying larger amounts, stocking up on essentials when they are on sale (and storing them in your newly uncluttered cabinets!), freezing specials on meats, fish, and poultry. For foods that must be bought more frequently, like fruits and vegetables, make out shopping lists ahead of time and try not to buy more than once a week. Consider having family members do the food shopping for you, or investigate having your groceries delivered. The same goes for pickup and/or delivery of dry cleaning, pharmaceutical needs, and other items.

Planning Rest Periods at Home

Taking daily rest periods is one of the most positive steps you can take to help reduce your risk of prematurity. Most women consider an afternoon nap a luxury, but during pregnancy it is actually therapeutic, particularly lying down on your left side, which increases the blood flow back to your heart (see Figure 12). Lying down every day will also decrease the amount of swelling in your legs and feet by increasing the blood flow to the kidneys and helping to eliminate excess fluids. And lying down reduces the amount of catecholamines, the "stress" hormones I talked about in Chapter 3, in your blood. Although it is preferable for you to sleep, lying down for at least twenty minutes at a time is still very beneficial. Consider having a foldaway bed set up downstairs (if you live in a two-story home) or stretching out on the couch or using a sofabed so that you can rest without having to climb stairs to the bedroom. If it's warm enough out, consider resting in a hammock. Between the fresh air and the "weightless" rocking sensation, you may find yourself napping in no time.

During the early and middle part of your pregnancy you may not feel tired enough to sleep, in which case

Figure 12

Resting position.

you may want to set aside some activities to do specifically during your daily rest periods, such as catching up on correspondence or reading. Toward the end of your pregnancy you will probably feel much more tired, and will probably look forward to these daily rest periods as a welcome opportunity to sleep for an hour or more.

Noise at home can hamper your ability to rest and is a subtle cause of stress you may not have even considered. It can lead to irritability, muscular tension, and insomnia. Turn radios and televisions down or off, lower the volume on your phone, and remind family members about loud conversations or shouting. Reduce the noise level at home and you will rest more comfortably.

Children and Rest Periods

Getting enough rest and lying down can significantly reduce the risk of prematurity. If you have preschool children at home, ask friends or neighbors to baby-sit for an hour or two daily, if possible. If you have older children at home, enroll them in an afterschool program or arrange for them to spend time at friends' homes so you can get some rest time. These arrangements don't always have to cost extra money: Twenty hours of baby-sitting (or thirty or forty!) would make an ideal practical shower gift from a favorite neighbor—you could even make it official with a "good for" coupon. Or try the barter system:

> Samantha, mother of four-year-old and thirteen-year-old girls, arranged for her neighbor to keep her children for two hours a day, five days a week, during the last month of her pregnancy. In exchange, Samantha promised to take her neighbor's thirteen-year-old daughter along with her own daughters on a two-week vacation to the beach later in the year.

Your Work Environment

Work outside the home has become an increasing part of most women's lives during the second half of this century, and the components of work are important factors influencing the risk of prematurity as well as low birthweight. For many women, working is not a choice but a necessity, and they cannot afford to reduce their hours or their pay, particularly with a baby on the way. In the second half of this chapter I will help you identify and modify stresses and risks in your work environment.

During the past thirty years, there have been major changes in women's participation in the American workforce, including the number of women working outside the home, working and having children, and working during their pregnancies. For example, between 1960 and 1993, the number of employed women in the United States more than doubled, increasing from 21.9 million to more than 58 million; by the year 2005, this figure is expected to reach 72 million (1). In 1993 nearly eight out of ten women were in the U.S. labor force, compared to five out of ten in 1970 and four out of ten in 1960. These changes are due to many factors, including changing educational and career opportunities for women, and family and economic considerations, which mean women must stay in the workforce continuously, with shorter absences for child-rearing. For example, the proportion of American families in which the husband works and the wife stays home has dropped from more than three out of five in 1960 to fewer than three out of ten in 1990, while the proportion of families in which both husband and wife work outside the home has risen from one out of four to one out of two during the same time period (2).

Unlike many of our mothers, who left the workforce once they became pregnant or when their pregnancy began to show, most women today continue to work late into their pregnancies or even until they go into labor. For example, during the decade between 1980 and 1990, the proportion of women in the labor force increased by about 12 percent, whereas the proportion of women who were in the labor force *and* who had also given birth within the previous year increased by 40 percent. In addition, according to recent studies by the U.S. Bureau of the Census, women are working longer into their pregnancies. For example, between 1961 and 1985, the proportion of women working during the last trimester of pregnancy increased by 50 percent, while the proportion working within one month of delivery more than doubled.

Employment itself has not been related to an increased risk of prematurity. Actually, some studies have shown that women who are employed outside the home are healthier and have a lower rate of prematurity compared to housewives (3–5); this has been termed "the healthy worker" effect. One theory offered to explain this difference is that employed women generally have more favorable demographic characteristics and fewer lifestyle risks (6). It is difficult to compare the results of the many studies done on work and pregnancy for several reasons. First, some studies have been conducted retrospectively, asking women to recall their working conditions after having given birth, while other studies have been conducted prospectively, asking women about their working conditions at the first prenatal visit and then following up at delivery. Second, some studies compare women working inside and outside the home without considering similarities in physical stresses. Third, some studies have included women from a wide variety of jobs and work environments with little basis for comparison. Despite these limitations, current scientific evidence suggests that individual aspects of work and the work environment may increase the risk of prematurity, including *standing, lifting, physical exertion, fatigue, irregular hours, noise,* and *stress.*

Do You Have a High-Stress Job?

In addition to becoming a larger proportion of the total workforce, women have also become a larger proportion of many occupations traditionally dominated by men. Although such fields as secretarial work and nursing are still predominately female, an increasing proportion of women are becoming bus drivers, computer programmers, lawyers, physicians, and telephone installers and repairers, to name a few. By joining some of these previously male-dominated occupations, women are now more frequently exposed to higher levels of physical exertion, noise, heavy lifting, longer and irregular work hours, and consequently, higher levels of mental and physical stress.

Several studies have identified *specific occupations* as being more prone to prematurity, by the nature of the overall work. For example, studies of physicians, particularly those still in training (interns and residents), have shown higher rates of premature labor, preterm birth, and low birthweight (7–9). Other occupations with higher preterm birth rates include nurses and other hospital personnel (10,11), active-duty military personnel (12–14), assembly-line workers, housekeepers and cleaning staff, and other occupations that involve long hours and physical effort. Also be aware that, despite the stereotype of the harried executive, in fact employees who have the least control over their work situations are often under the most work-related stress.

Does Your Job Require Much Standing?

As discussed in Chapter 3, *standing,* particularly for more than four hours at a time, is a risk factor for prematurity and complications associated with prematurity, such as high blood pressure (10,11,15–21). Studies have shown that the increased risk due to standing ranges from 26 percent (19) to 56 to 73 percent (11,15,21), to more than 2.7-fold (16). In comparing occupations that are primarily standing, sedentary, or active, one large study reported the incidence of premature birth to be 7.7 percent, 4.2 percent, and 2.8 percent, respectively, and the incidence of low birthweight to be 5.5 percent, 4.0 percent, and 4.0 percent, respectively. Small-for-gestational age (SGA, birthweight less than the 10th percentile for gestational age, see Chapter 1) is also associated with standing, with a 32 percent increased risk for manual workers versus office workers, and a greater than 2.5-fold increased risk for SGA and preterm (15).

As discussed in Chapter 3, much of the risk involved with standing centers around blockage of the blood flow to and from the uterus, particularly during the third trimester. As the uterus grows larger, it compresses the uterine arteries and veins against the bony pelvis, blocking blood flow back to the heart. As discussed previously, prolonged periods of quiet standing will cause the uterus to begin to contract to lift itself off the pelvis and restore normal circulation (22–26), an effect known as the *vena cava syndrome*. These contractions, as discussed before, can lead to premature labor and preterm birth. Remember, the American Medical Association recommends that you don't stand for more than four hours at a time after 24 weeks' gestation, and no more than thirty minutes in an hour after 32 weeks' gestation (27). Try some of the same measures recommended at home for your work environment. Use chairs and stools at workstations and change from standing to sitting activities whenever possible. If you commute by train or bus, be careful how long you stand going to and from work. Don't be timid about asking a fellow commuter to give you a seat—you *need* to sit down!

Does Your Job Involve Much Physical Exertion?

Physical exertion, including lifting and carrying, is an important risk factor frequently cited in studies of prematurity (10–15,28,29). As discussed in Chapter 3, lifting and carrying increase pressure on the uterus and therefore the risk of premature contractions. The frequency and weight of lifting are also important factors, with repetitive worse than intermittent, and heavy worse than light. (See pages 52 and 53 for improper and proper lifting techniques.) Among military personnel employed in the highest levels of physical activity, the risk of preterm birth was increased by 70 to 75 percent (12) and by 500 percent compared to military personnel employed at lower levels of physical activity (13). Occupations that involve a great deal of physical exertion, such as manual work (15), cleaning (11), assembly-line work (21), and nursing (10,15,29), have all been associated with significantly higher levels of prematurity and low birthweight. As discussed in Chapter 3, the American Medical Association recommends that pregnant women should not do repetitive lifting of more than 50 pounds beyond 20 weeks' gestation, and no more than 24 to 50 pounds beyond 24 weeks' gestation (27). They also recommend that pregnant women should not do intermittent lifting of more than 50 pounds beyond 30 weeks' gestation.

As I discussed earlier in this chapter, part of reducing your physical effort at work involves reducing clutter and becoming more organized. If ever you needed an excuse to streamline your office or job, this is it—blame it on the baby! Get rid of clutter on your desk, organize your files, stock up on supplies you use all the time so they will be at hand. Think about the nature of your work and become as efficient as possible. Instead of making a dozen trips to the copier in a day, make one or two. Instead of running up and down the stairs to check on something, use the phone. Stock extra paper for the printer in your office. Replenish supplies on a weekly basis. Become as organized at work as you have become at home!

The dangers of physical exertion during pregnancy are twofold: the repetitive or intermittent increase in pressure on the uterus and the resulting fatigue. Your goal is to minimize both risk factors at work, either by modifying how you do your job, or by changing to another kind of job during your pregnancy. If your work does require much physical exertion, talk to your supervisor or boss about modifying your work or changing to another type of work while pregnant. It's in everyone's best interest to prevent prematurity; call upon your obstetrician as your workplace advocate, if you have to.

Do You Work More Than Eight Hours Per Day or More Than Forty Hours Per Week?

Irregular or *long working hours* (more than thirty-five or forty hours per week, or more than eight hours per day) are also risk factors for prematurity (10,28–30). If you work nonstandard work schedules, such as evenings, nights, or rotating shifts, you may experience a disruption in your biological or circadian rhythms, which, in turn, can influence the course of your pregnancy (31). Many occupations require twenty-four-hour operation, such as manufacturing, utilities, protective and health services (police, fire and rescue, and hospitals), transportation, and communications. If your job requires working shifts, you're not alone: Approximately one out of five Americans is a shift worker, with 10 percent working nights, 15 percent rotating shifts, and the remainder splitting shifts or evenings (31). The amount of shift work varies greatly by industry, ranging from as little as 6 percent in finance, insurance, and real estate to as much as nearly 48 percent in restaurants; this latter industry also has the highest proportion of rotating shifts (12.5 percent).

The most common work schedule in the United States is eight hours per day, five days a week on a single shift, with two days off. Shifts can vary from eight to twelve hours, and with the compressed workweek, forty hours of work is done in fewer than five days. The compressed workweek with twelve-hour shifts is common in the chemical, petroleum, and steel industries, as well as in nursing and computer operations.

Among dual-income couples, at least one spouse in one out of four couples without children and one out of three with children works a nonstandard shift. One-half of all young couples with children under the age of five include at least one spouse that works a nonstandard shift. The reasons for shift work may be both voluntary and nonvoluntary. Voluntary reasons include better childcare and family member care arrangements, higher pay, and more opportunities for education. Involuntary reasons include the inability to get any other job and the schedule being a requirement of the position. According to the Bureau of Labor Statistics, only 28 percent of individuals working nonstandard shifts do so voluntarily; 72 percent do so involuntarily, and for nine out of ten, the schedule is a requirement of the job.

Humans are naturally diurnal beings, geared toward active wakefulness during the day and sleep at night. Women who must work shifts fight this natural diurnal trend, resulting in disruption of circadian rhythms and sleep patterns, which can cause fatigue and stress. Sleep cycles, the release of hormones, and the menstrual cycle are three examples of physiologic events that occur in biological rhythms, and that are very susceptible to circadian disruption. *Fatigue* in general has been shown in various studies to be associated with prematurity (10,17,21,28); the chronic fatigue and stress from disrupted circadian rhythms may also contribute to your risk of miscarriage, low birthweight, and preterm birth (28,31–33).

If you do work shifts, speak with your supervisor about modifying your schedule to reduce the number of rotating shifts, or the possibility of remaining on one shift for the duration of your pregnancy. Working more than eight hours per day is also a strong risk factor for prematurity. If you are currently working more than eight hours per day, cut down the number of hours you work to eight or fewer, perhaps by working a half-shift on another day. This is especially important if your work involves considerable lifting, carrying, standing, driving, or results in fatigue. Again, use your obstetrician as your advocate in negotiating to reduce these workplace risks for prematurity.

If your work involves using a computer for long hours at a time, take extra measures to reduce fatigue and strain, such as changing positions and taking breaks frequently, using glare-reducing devices and movable keyboards, and doing stretching exercises every hour or so. Eyestrain is a common cause of fatigue among individuals who use computers and who do a lot of desk work. Try alternating the amount of time you spend using your computer or typewriter with running errands around your office, or even tasks that involve writing by hand. Make sure you use a supporting office chair, preferably one with good lower-back support and armrests. Lower your keyboard to minimize the strain on your wrists and hands. Use adequate lighting and make sure there is sufficient ventilation. Keep nonperishable snacks in your desk or bring fruit from home for your breaks. If possible, elevate your feet on a box or stepstool while typing or working at your desk.

Remember those rest breaks you used to take when you were in kindergarten? Those little rugs you brought to school and would pull out so that you could lie down on the floor for a nap? They were a good idea then, and they're a good idea now! If you work in your own office, or can borrow someone else's, use it for your rest breaks. Bring a small blanket or mat to work and spread it out on the floor in your office or the office of a friend. Lie down to rest (preferably on your left side to increase blood flow to the heart), and to do any other activity that is part of your work (see Figure 13 for correct positioning). For example, if the mail comes twice a day, lie down on your mat to sort through it. Make or return phone calls. If you need to put labels on file folders or organize papers, spread them out on the floor and lie down on your side to work on them.

As discussed in Chapter 3, *stress,* both physical and mental, may result from these various work factors, and

Figure 13

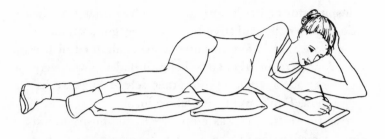

A comfortable position for working while resting.

may explain much of their physical effects on pregnancy. Physical and mental stress result in an increased production of the catecholamine "stress" hormones *epinephrine* and *norepinephrine* (34,35). Norepinephrine excretion is increased during exposure to cold, increases in blood pressure, and aggressive reactions, indicating its importance in temperature-controlling and circulatory mechanisms. Changing from a recumbent (lying down) to an erect position causes a threefold increase in norepinephrine excretion, indicating that standing causes a certain amount of circulatory stress (36). During heavy physical work norepinephrine excretion may be increased more than 100-fold, for the same reasons (37,38). Epinephrine excretion increases with mental or emotional stress, such as noise, pain, anxiety, discomfort, apprehension, oral and written examinations, and problem solving. In a recent pilot study of pregnant physicians and intensive care unit nurses, catecholamine levels were found to increase by 58 percent during workdays compared to nonwork-days (39).

Emily, a thirty-five-year-old nurse and mother of two preschoolers, worked twelve-hour shifts every Saturday and Sunday in the emergency room of a large urban hospital during her last pregnancy. The working conditions were noisy and stressful; she rarely got to sit down for more than a few minutes, usually didn't finish a meal, and frequently had to help lift patients who were unconscious or couldn't move themselves. At 32 weeks' gestation, Emily went into labor during a particularly stressful shift. She was admitted to the hospital and given medications to try to stop her contractions, but within a few hours she gave birth. Her son weighed four pounds at birth and spent a week in newborn intensive care and another two weeks in the newborn nursery.

Is Your Workplace Noisy?

Noise at work is an important risk factor you may not be immediately aware of. Lower or turn off radios, avoid working next to noisy machines or near busy thoroughfares. Carpeted floors and curtain or draperies muffle considerable amounts of noise—move into an environment with these, if possible. Take work to a quieter environment when you can: Put your feet up, a pillow at your lower back, and enjoy the quiet!

Even if your job is not physically demanding, you may be exhausted at the end of the day from the mental stress. Balancing conflicts among employees, meeting deadlines, dealing with unexpected delays, changes, emergencies, and tensions can all result in physical symptoms of stress: headaches, stomachaches, nervous twitches, irritability, and inability to concentrate.

Assessing Your Work Risks

As you have done with the previous chapter, use the Checklist 2 at the end of this chapter to document your work risks, and try to modify those you can. As discussed in Chapter 3, try to reduce the amount of standing you do at work, either by using chairs and stools or by moving to another workstation or work area. Reduce the amount of standing you do while commuting back and forth from work. If lifting heavy objects is part of your job, discuss a temporary change of duties with your supervisor to reduce your risks. It may be necessary to enlist the help of your obstetrician or healthcare provider if you cannot work out a modified arrangement with your boss (see Chapter 8). Reduce those factors you can, such as noise and long or irregular work hours. Rest periods are extremely important, particularly in a recumbent (lying down) position. Try to find ways to reduce or better manage the mental stress of your job.

> Beth, a thirty-seven-year-old professional baker, was pregnant with her second child. Her first pregnancy was fifteen years ago, when she was in college. Divorced from the father of her first child and remarried, both she and her life were very different this second time around. First, she was older and got much more tired by the end of the day than she remembered feeling with her first pregnancy. Second, her daily work was much more stressful and demanding than when she was in college: Her work environment was frequently hot and noisy. To reduce her risks of prematurity, at 28 weeks' gestation Beth took several important preventive

steps: She cut down the number of hours she worked per day from eight to six; she cut down the number of days she worked from five to four; she changed her work hours to when the kitchens were less busy, to reduce stress and exposure to noise; and she sat instead of stood whenever possible. Beth worked this modified schedule for eight weeks, then stayed home for the last two weeks of her pregnancy. At 38 weeks' gestation, she gave birth to a healthy 7-pound 6-ounce baby girl.

Use the checklist on page 91 to document your risk factors in your home and work environments, as well as those you've been able to modify or eliminate. Remember, even small steps add up. You may find that you enjoy your day-to-day life much better once you have identified and reduced daily stresses. You may even decide to stick with this program after you have delivered!

Checklist 2. Home and Workplace Risk Factors

	Nonmodifiable	Modifiable	Modified
HOME ENVIRONMENT			
Stair climbing at home			
Lifting at home			
Carrying at home			
Standing at home			
Noise at home			
Driving (home and chores)			
WORK ENVIRONMENT	*Nonmodifiable*	*Modifiable*	*Modified*
High-risk occupation			
Standing-commuting to and from work			
Standing at work			
Lifting at work			
Physical exertion at work			
Irregular work hours			
Shift work			
Long work hours (>8 hrs/day)			
Long workweek (>35 or 40 hrs/week)			
Fatigue at work			
Noise at work			
Stress at work			
Driving (at work and commuting)			

5

Your Lifestyle: Risks and Rewards

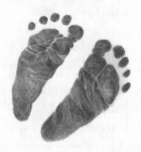

THE NEXT SET of risk factors we're going to evaluate are ones that involve personal choices in your everyday life, both at home and at work. These risk factors include: alcohol use, smoking, caffeine intake, the use of medications and drugs, and recreational exercise. Your doctor may or may not ask you about these factors, but they are still very important to consider in evaluating your overall risk. Each of these risk factors is modifiable; it's in your power to change some of the ways you lead your life to better your chances of having a healthy baby.

Do You Drink Alcohol?

In the United States, approximately seven out of ten adults consume alcohol (1). Although men drink alcohol more frequently and in larger amounts, the proportion of women who drink alcohol has been steadily increasing. A recent national survey by the Centers for Disease Control estimated the incidence of alcohol consumption among women of childbearing age, and classified women by the number of drinks consumed during the preceding month as nondrinker (none); light (thirty or fewer); moderate (thirty-one to fifty-nine); heavy (sixty or more); and binge drinker (five or more drinks on one occasion)(2). This survey reported that about 50 percent were nondrinkers, 45 percent light drinkers, 3 percent moderate drinkers, and 2 percent heavy drinkers. Among all drinkers in the survey, 21 percent reported binge drinking. At the time of the interview, about 4 percent of the respondents were pregnant; of these, 13.4 percent reported light drinking, 0.1 percent moderate, 0.3 percent heavy, and 1.3 percent binge drinking.

If even the thought of taking a drink makes you sick, you're not alone. Most women report an aversion to alcohol during pregnancy, even if they drank regularly before becoming pregnant. For example, in a study of dietary cravings and aversions in pregnancy, one-fourth to one-third of women who drank alcohol regularly before pregnancy reduced their intake during the first half of pregnancy because of a loss of the taste for it or the nausea induced by it (3). Data from the Centers for Disease Control's Pregnancy Nutrition Surveillance System, which monitors health practices and pregnancy outcomes on over three hundred thousand women in the United States, indicate that while about 14 percent of women drank alcohol before pregnancy, only 4.3 percent continue during pregnancy (4). Alcohol consumption during pregnancy can have serious and permanent adverse effects for your unborn baby; let me tell you why.

Women Metabolize Alcohol Differently

About one-fourth to one-third of the alcohol ingested is absorbed in the stomach (gastric absorption); the remainder is absorbed in the small intestine. Gastric absorption is increased by the presence of carbonated fluids, and delayed by coldness and the presence of other foods, particularly those high in protein, fat, or sugar, whereas the absorption of alcohol in the small intestine occurs very rapidly regardless of the presence of food. Men and women differ in their ability to absorb alcohol, with women having less gastric absorption and more rapid and complete absorption in the small intestine (5). Because of this difference, women are more susceptible to the effects of alcohol, more likely to have a higher blood alcohol content (become drunk quicker) from the same amount, and suffer more long-term physical damage from its effects (6–8).

Alcohol disrupts the body's normal hormonal and metabolic balance, resulting in decreased fertility for both men and women. In men, heavy drinking can result in impotence, decreased libido (sex drive), as well as lowered sperm count. The metabolism of alcohol diverts important enzymes from their functions, and the results can lead to such consequences as reduced production of sperm and male hormones (testosterone). In women, heavy alcohol intake can result in disruption of the menstrual cycle, as well as a loss of libido (9,10). Alcohol consumption has also been linked to *spontaneous abortions,* with the risk paralleling intake. In a recent study of over forty-seven thousand women in Canada, the risk of spontaneous abortions increased 11 percent with one to two drinks per week, 23 percent with three to six drinks per week, 47 percent with seven to twenty drinks per week, and 82 percent with twenty-one or more drinks per week (11).

Alcohol has both *teratogenic* (causes birth defects) and *embryotoxic* (causes spontaneous abortions) effects. In 1968 French researchers reported a pattern of abnormalities among children of alcoholic women; these included growth retardation, mental retardation, and congenital anomalies (especially cleft palate and cardiac malformations)(12). This pattern of abnormalities was also described by other researchers, and in 1973 it was termed the *fetal alcohol syndrome,* or *FAS* (13). Children with a milder form of FAS, but who show some aspects of the syndrome are classified as having *fetal alcohol effects,* or *FAE.* The incidence of FAS is estimated to be about 1.9 per 1,000 live births, and FAE about 3 to 5 per 1,000 live births (14–16). Among alcoholic women, the incidence of FAS is estimated to be as high as 25 per 1,000 live births, and FAE about 90 per 1,000 live births (16). FAS is the leading cause of mental retardation in the Western world, surpassing Down's syndrome and cerebral palsy (14).

Back in the early 1970s, when I had a maternal nutrition clinic at the Columbia-Presbyterian Medical Center in New York City, few women knew about the relationship between drinking and FAS. Most women had never even heard of FAS. I saw so many children born with this syndrome that I wrote about it in the nursing literature (17). In 1978 I was asked by a U.S. senator who had read my article to testify before a senate subcommittee on my experiences with FAS in New York City. This was when the government was first considering requiring labels on all alcoholic beverages warning pregnant women of the risks of FAS. Since then these labels have became mandatory.

The effects of alcohol during pregnancy are related to the toxic effects of alcohol itself, its by-products, and resulting nutritional imbalances. Because alcohol is soluble in both water and lipid (fat), it passes through all membranes in the body, interfering with cell division and protein synthesis, the two most common and critical processes occurring in your unborn baby. This is why alcohol use during pregnancy causes birth defects and mental retardation, as well as an overall reduction in growth (18). The effect is dose-related, although there is no proven safe lower limit of intake (19–21). The metabolism of alcohol is very different for your unborn baby than it is for you, his or her mother. The amniotic fluid around your baby acts as a reservoir for alcohol, and because the baby lacks the necessary enzymes to metabolize it, he or she is exposed to it long after it has been cleared from your blood supply (22–24). In addition, alcohol may be directly toxic to the placenta, resulting in a kind of "selective" fetal malnutrition, independent of the nutrition provided by the mother (25).

In a recent follow-up study of sixty-one adolescents and adults who had been diagnosed with FAS as infants, Streissguth and co-workers concluded that,

> . . . fetal alcohol syndrome is not just a childhood disorder. There is a predictable, long-term progression of the disorder into adulthood in which maladaptive behaviors present the greatest challenge to treatment. Gestational exposure to alcohol can cause a wide spectrum of disabilities that have lifelong physical, mental, and behavioral implications. (26)

Pregnancy is the perfect time to stop drinking alcohol. Because there is no safe lower limit, it is prudent to stop completely. This is one of the few risk factors that is completely under your control. If you are having trouble quitting, get help from a friend, member of the clergy, support group, or other source. Remember, a baby is made only once, and he or she is counting on you!

Do You Smoke?

Cigarette smoking is the single most important preventable cause of death in the United States, and a major factor in many illnesses, including pregnancy complications (27). Since 1964 the U.S. Surgeon General's annual report has focused on the health consequences associated with smoking (28). Based on estimates from the Centers for Disease Control, more than 46 million adults in the United States are currently smokers (29). More than one out of five women smoke. Those who do are at increased risk for chronic lung diseases, such as lung cancer and chronic pulmonary disease, and if they also use oral contraceptives, myocardial infarction (heart attack) (30).

Like drinking alcohol, smoking during pregnancy is a completely modifiable risk factor. In the United States today, about one in five women smokes during pregnancy, averaging about eighteen cigarettes per day (31). Research on smoking has shown adverse effects on fertility, spontaneous abortions, pregnancy complications, birthweight, and prematurity. Many of the studies that evaluated the effects of caffeine on pregnancy outcome reported a strong correlation between coffee intake and smoking (32–34). These two factors together may be additive or even multiplicative in their adverse effects on conception and the baby's health.

Ectopic pregnancy, the implantation of the fertilized egg in the Fallopian tube, is a complication documented to occur two to four times more frequently among smokers (36,37). Nicotine, one of the thousands of components in cigarette smoke, has been shown to reduce the motility of the Fallopian tubes in animal studies (35).

Spontaneous abortion, pregnancy loss before 20 weeks' gestation, occurs 20 to 80 percent more frequently among smokers, resulting in a spontaneous abortion rate of 18 to 27 percent for smokers (38,39). Data from a study of more than forty-seven thousand women in Canada who gave birth between 1982 and 1984 reported an increased risk of spontaneous abortions of 7 percent with one to nine cigarettes per day, 22 percent with ten to nineteen cigarettes per day, and 68 percent with twenty or more per day (11). This study concluded that 11 percent of all spontaneous abortions were due to smoking. A recent study of women who conceived by in vitro fertilization reported that the rate of spontaneous abortion was twice as great for smokers compared to nonsmokers (42.1 percent versus 18.9 percent)(40). In addition, compared to those of nonsmokers, the spontaneous abortions of smokers are 40 percent more likely to be genetically normal (41). Studies have also shown that among men smoking results in impaired sperm concentration, motility, and structure (42,43).

Many studies have linked smoking during pregnancy with placental complications, lower birthweight, premature rupture of membranes (PROM), prematurity, and increased infant death. The primary culprits in cigarette smoke are carbon monoxide and nicotine. These substances rob oxygen from the unborn baby, and may also adversely affect the fetus's developing respiratory, gastrointestinal, genital, urinary, and central nervous systems (28,44). Smoking causes severe changes in the placenta, including alterations in its structure and function, and an acceleration in its aging. (The placenta ages naturally during the course of pregnancy, but premature or accelerated aging can compromise its ability to function effectively.) As a result, the placenta of a woman who smokes is less able to function adequately, resulting in a decrease in the amount of oxygen and nutrients transferred to the unborn baby. Bleeding and placental complications are 50 percent more common among women who smoke, including placenta previa and abruptio placentae (see Chapter 2)(45–47). Several studies have demonstrated a relationship between smoking and premature rupture of membranes (PROM) (see Chapter 2)(48–50). A recent large study in Boston reported that women who smoked during pregnancy had a 2.2-fold higher risk of PROM compared to nonsmokers, and this risk increased with the number of cigarettes smoked per day (51).

More than thirty-five years ago research linked maternal smoking with prematurity (52). Since then many other studies have confirmed this initial observation: smokers are 20 to 50 percent more likely to deliver prematurely compared to nonsmokers (27,47,53–56). A recent study from Finland reported that women who smoked during pregnancy had a 2.4-fold increased risk of prematurity (57).

Maternal smoking also adversely affects *birthweight*. Among infants born at term, smoking reduces birthweight by 150 to 300 grams (5 to 10 ounces), with the effect being more severe among underweight women with poor weight gain (58)(see Table 4). Smokers have a 2-fold increased risk of having a low birthweight infant and a 2- to 4-fold increase of having a growth-retarded infant (small-for-gestational age), whether born at term or preterm (53,46,47,56,59,60). Women who smoked before pregnancy and quit or cut down by the first trimester reduced their risk of having a low-birthweight infant (53,61). Likewise, women who cut down from the first to the second trimester also reduced their risk of having a low-birthweight infant, but to a lesser extent. A study of nearly 350,000 births in Washington state reported that among smokers, the risk of low birthweight increases with the mother's age, rising from 43 percent for ages sixteen to seventeen to 263 percent for women over forty (62).

Table 4. Birthweight of Term Infants by Maternal Prepregnancy Weight, Weight Gain, and Smoking Habits*

Prepregnancy weight and smoking groups	Gestational Weight Gain				
	<16 lb	16–20 lb	21–25 lb	26–35 lb	>36 lb
Underweight					
Nonsmoker	6 lb 6 oz	6 lb 12 oz	7 lb 2 oz	7 lb 6 oz	7 lb 10 oz
Smoker	5 lb 12 oz	6 lb 2 oz	6 lb 11 oz	6 lb 15 oz	7 lb 4 oz
Difference	– 10 oz	– 10 oz	– 7 oz	– 7 oz	– 7 oz
Normal weight					
Nonsmoker	6 lb 12 oz	7 lb 1 oz	7 lb 8 oz	7 lb 9 oz	7 lb 14 oz
Smoker	6 lb 6 oz	6 lb 11 oz	6 lb 14 oz	7 lb 3 oz	7 lb 7 oz
Difference	– 6 oz	– 6 oz	– 10 oz	– 6 oz	– 7 oz
Overweight					
Nonsmoker	7 lb 4 oz	7 lb 9 oz	7 lb 11 oz	7 lb 13 oz	8 lb
Smoker	7 lb 2 oz	7 lb 6 oz	7 lb 6 oz	7 lb 6 oz	7 lb 11 oz
Difference	– 2 oz	– 3 oz	– 5 oz	– 7 oz	– 5 oz

*Adapted from the 1980 National Natality Survey from the National Center for Health Statistics.

The reduction in birthweight is most likely caused by several mechanisms, including the lack of oxygen due to carbon monoxide, vascular changes in the placenta due to nicotine, decreased transport of nutrients by the damaged placenta, and decreased availability of zinc. Another component of cigarette smoke is cadmium, a zinc antagonist. Low levels of zinc have been linked to growth retardation (63,64). As a result of these pregnancy complications, the rates of death during the neonatal period are much higher for infants of smokers. In addition, the risk of sudden infant death syndrome (SIDS) is also much higher among infants of smokers (65).

Smoking also has indirect adverse effects, such as causing a variety of nutritional imbalances, which can set the stage for pregnancy complications. For example, smokers require more than three times the Recommended Dietary Allowance (RDA) of vitamin C (60 milligrams/day) to maintain the same blood levels of vitamin C as nonsmokers (66). Smokers (and their newborns) also have lower levels of vitamins A, B6, E, and folic acid compared to nonsmokers (66–69).

The 1990 report from the Surgeon General estimated that *20 percent of low-birthweight infants, 8 percent of preterm births, and 5 percent of all perinatal deaths could be prevented by eliminating smoking during pregnancy* (27). Ideally, you should stop smoking before conception, or, at latest, during the first trimester. Although about one out of five women do quit before their first prenatal visit (27), less than two out of twenty-five give up smoking later in pregnancy (70). Among the general population, 65 percent of individuals who stop smoking relapse within three months, 10 percent relapse within three to six months, but only 3 percent relapse after six to twelve months (27). It has been suggested that women who successfully quit for the nine months of pregnancy may have a low relapse rate (70). If you are a smoker, now is the time to quit or at least cut down substantially. In addition, improve your nutritional status by eating a better diet and taking a multivitamin supplement, particularly one with additional vitamin C, B vitamins, zinc, and folic acid (see Chapter 6, p. 156). Also, be sure you gain toward the upper range of the recommended weight gain for your prepregnancy weight (see Chapter 6). Pregnancy is the best reason you will ever have to stop smoking!

How Much Coffee or Tea Do You Drink?

Caffeine is the predominant active component in coffee, responsible for its stimulating effect. Although the majority of caffeine in our food supply comes from coffee, other foods, including colas and chocolate, also contribute a substantial amount (see Table 5).

The effects of caffeine on reproduction are not completely known. Because caffeine has a chemical structure similar to DNA, our genetic building blocks, it has the potential to interfere with cell division and metabolism. Caffeine does cross over to the developing baby, and the metabolism of this substance is three times slower in pregnant women than in nonpregnant women (71). Animal studies from the 1960s and 1970s have shown an association between caffeine intake and birth defects, spontaneous abortion, and lowered birthweight (72–75). On the basis of these studies, both the

Table 5. Dietary Sources of Caffeine*

Source	Amount	Caffeine (mg.)
Brewed coffee	6 fluid oz	90–100
Ground coffee	1 Tbsp	
Chocolate chips, semisweet	6 oz	
Coca-Cola	12 fluid oz	40–60
Cherry Coca-Cola	12 fluid oz	
Diet Coke	12 fluid oz	
Diet Cherry Coke	12 fluid oz	
Dr. Pepper	12 fluid oz	
Diet Dr. Pepper	12 fluid oz	
Diet-Rite Cola	12 fluid oz	
Tab	12 fluid oz	
Mello Yello	12 fluid oz	
Mountain Dew	12 fluid oz	
Powdered instant coffee	1 rounded tsp	
Carnation Instant Breakfast, coffee	1 packet	30–40
Pepsi-Cola	12 fluid oz	
Pepsi Light	12 fluid oz	
Diet Pepsi	12 fluid oz	
Brewed tea	6 fluid oz	
Instant tea	1 tsp	
Hershey's Special Dark Chocolate	1.45-oz bar	
Cherry RC Cola	12 fluid oz	10–20
RC Cola	12 fluid oz	
Semisweet chocolate	1 oz	
Chocolate chips	¼ cup	
Nestlé Crunch bar	1.4-oz bar	
Hershey's Golden Almond bar	3.2-oz bar	
Mars Milky Way bar	2.1-oz bar	
Hershey's Kit Kat Wafer	1.6-oz bar	<10
Hershey's Krackel bar	1.65-oz bar	
Hershey's Mr. Goodbar	1.75-oz bar	
Reese's Peanut Butter Cups	1.8-oz bar	
Hershey's Rolos	1.94 oz	
Brownies	1 oz	
Devil's food cake	¹⁄₁₂ cake	
Chocolate chip cookies	2 medium	
Chocolate pudding	½ cup	

*Adapted from J.A.T. Pennington, *Food Values of Portions Commonly Used*. 16th ed. Philadelphia: JB Lippincott, 1994.

Food and Drug Administration and the National Academy of Sciences have cautioned pregnant women to limit their intake of coffee and caffeine-containing beverages and foods (76,77). During the past fifteen years many more studies have been conducted regarding the effects of caffeine intake on reproduction. Although the results are not absolutely conclusive, they do demonstrate several points.

The effect of coffee consumption on *delaying conception* has been evaluated (78–82). One study estimated that the risk of being unable to become pregnant within one year was 28 percent for women who consumed more than thirty-one cups of coffee per month compared to 6 percent for those who weren't coffee drinkers (78). A second study reported that women who were having trouble becoming pregnant were almost twice as likely to be heavy coffee drinkers (four or more cups per day) compared to those who had no difficulty conceiving (79). A third study showed that the average time to conception was longer for women who drank four or more cups of coffee per day (6.7 months) compared to nondrinkers (4.8 months) (80). The relationship between caffeine intake and delayed conception is dose-related, increasing by 39 percent with intakes of 150 milligrams or lower, 88 percent with intakes between 150 and 300 milligrams, and more than 2.2-fold for intakes over 300 milligrams per day (81).

The association between coffee consumption and the rate of spontaneous abortions has also been investigated (11,83–85). One study of over three thousand women reported a 70 percent increase in spontaneous abortions between 8 and 26 weeks' gestation in moderate coffee drinkers compared to nondrinkers (84). An-

other study reported a two-thirds increase in spontaneous abortions among drinkers versus nondrinkers
(83). A third study reported a 50 percent higher incidence of spontaneous abortions with heavy coffee consumption (six or more cups per day) (85).

Many studies have examined the relationship between coffee consumption and *birth defects* (83,86–92).
In studies ranging from Boston to Philadelphia,
Toronto to Finland, based on interviews with thousands of women just after delivery, no association between coffee consumption and birth defects could be
demonstrated. The incidence of birth defects was low
among both coffee drinkers and non-coffee drinkers.
Data on all birth defects from ten European countries
indicate that there is little correlation between coffee
consumption and birth defects (91). Two studies, one
from Japan and one from Belgium, did show that the
incidence of birth defects was about twofold higher
among women who were heavy coffee drinkers (eight
or more cups per day) compared to those who were
light coffee drinkers (one to two cups per day) or nondrinkers (83,90).

Other studies have examined the effect of coffee
consumption on reducing birthweight and the incidence of low birthweight. The majority of studies
show an inverse relationship between coffee consumption and birthweight (33,34,83,87,93–97). The increased risk of low birthweight babies ranged from 20
percent (87) to more than 460 percent (33) for drinkers
of more than three cups of coffee per day. One study,
which followed women from within twenty-one days
after conception to delivery, reported a higher proportion of babies with birthweights below the 10th per-

centile (small-for-gestational age, see Chapter 1) born to women consuming more than 300 milligrams of caffeine per day (three or more six-ounce cups of coffee per day), but the relationship disappeared after taking into account the effect of smoking (34). Overall, coffee consumption does appear to have an effect on birthweight, particularly at higher levels of intake.

Caffeine may reduce birthweight indirectly by decreasing both the mother's body weight before pregnancy and the amount of weight she gains during pregnancy through its actions on metabolism. Clinical studies have shown caffeine to have anorectic (appetite-reducing), thermogenic (increase body temperature), and lipolytic (breakdown of body fat) effects in humans, and for these reasons it is frequently a component in weight-reduction medications (98–101). Other studies have found that caffeine reduces blood flow to the placenta as well as increasing maternal blood pressure and fetal heart rate, suggesting additional indirect explanations for the reduction in fetal growth (102,103). Caffeine intake also results in an increase in catecholamines, which, as discussed in Chapter 3, reduce blood flow to the uterus (104,105).

Prematurity has also been evaluated in regard to coffee intake. The results are not as clear as in other outcomes, but the findings of most studies suggest that prematurity is not associated with coffee intake (33,53,96,97,106). A recent study of over forty thousand women in Canada found a slight increase in the risk of prematurity with five to nine cups of coffee per day, and a 24 percent increased risk with ten or more cups per day (53). A recent study evaluated the association between premature rupture of membranes

(PROM) and coffee intake (51). The findings indicated that women who consumed three or more cups of coffee daily during the first trimester had a 2.2-fold increased risk of PROM compared to women who drank two cups or less per day; this risk paralleled increasing coffee consumption.

The amount of caffeine in coffee depends on the method of preparation, with an average six-ounce cup of brewed or percolated coffee containing about 100 milligrams of caffeine. Brewed tea contains about 40 milligrams per six-ounce cup, colas about 30 to 50 milligrams per twelve ounces. If you drink more than a cup or two of coffee or tea a day, it's a good idea to determine the size of your cup or mug. To do this, fill it with water, then pour that water into a glass measuring cup. If your coffee cup holds eight ounces, and you brew your coffee average strength, you're getting about 130 milligrams of caffeine. If you brew your coffee strong, you may be getting as much as 180 to 200 milligrams in your eight-ounce cup, and as much as 300 milligrams if you have a twelve-ounce mug! If you like to drink a lot of coffee, try mixing half decaffeinated espresso with half regular coffee to keep the rich full flavor while cutting down on the caffeine. Of course, to cut down even more, you can switch to decaffeinated coffee or decaffeinated tea.

Caffeine is also a common ingredient in many nonprescription and prescription medications, including over-the-counter preparations for colds, headaches, allergies, antidrowsiness, and premenstrual symptoms. For example, the caffeine content of some common medications per tablet is: Cafergot and No-Doz (100 milligrams); Fiorinal (40 milligrams); APC (aspirin, phenacetin, caffeine), Darvon Compound, Vanquish, Cope, Empirin Compound, Bromo-Seltzer, and Anacin (32 milligrams); Dristan and Sinarest (30 milligrams). Before you take any medication during pregnancy, check with your doctor, but keep in mind that even he or she may not realize there is caffeine in these and other common medications. If you have any question whether something you're taking contains caffeine, ask your pharmacist.

Based on the current scientific evidence, it has recently been advised that women limit their coffee consumption to no more than two cups per day, particularly women who have had difficulty becoming pregnant, or who are at risk for having a premature or low-birthweight infant (107).

Do You Take Any Medications or Drugs?

Any drug you take—including something as seemingly innocuous as a vitamin or an aspirin tablet—even before you're pregnant, can affect the health of your unborn child. If you are planning on becoming pregnant, discuss any medications you're currently taking with your doctor. Unless the medications are absolutely crucial to your health, he or she will probably advise you to taper the dosage and discontinue them. The use of some drugs during the first trimester (first 14 weeks after conception) can cause birth defects; some can have other adverse effects. If you are currently pregnant, check with your doctor about anything you are taking, including over-the-counter medications, even aspirin.

Illegal drugs, such as cocaine, heroin, and marijuana, all have adverse effects on the unborn child, ranging from low birthweight and prematurity to death. These are dangerous substances even when you are not pregnant, but when you are pregnant you are risking your own health and that of your unborn child. If ever you needed an excuse to quit, now is the time. Do it for yourself and your baby, and get help if you need it.

Do You Exercise?

Like the other three factors discussed in this chapter, recreational exercise is something *completely under your control*. I'm sure you know women who consider running to catch a bus exercise and others who feel guilty if they don't run at least five miles every day! Recreational exercise during pregnancy is a very important factor to consider because, like the physical exertion at home or at work, it causes the release of catecholamines—stress hormones—which, in turn, can increase your risk of prematurity (108-111). You may have read in health and fitness magazines recently about "getting into shape for delivery." This concept may actually cause more harm than good, by focusing on your overall physical fitness rather than on how physical activity increases your risk of prematurity. You can always get into shape, but when you're pregnant, the intensity, duration, and frequency of your physical activity can dramatically increase your risk of prematurity.

Physical changes in your body as a result of pregnancy may interfere with your ability to engage safely

---

The American College of Obstetricians and Gynecologists Contraindications to Exercise During Pregnancy*

- Pregnancy-induced hypertension

- Premature rupture of membranes

- Preterm labor during a prior and/or current pregnancy

- Incompetent cervix with or without surgical treatment

- Second- or third-trimester bleeding

- Intrauterine growth retardation

* Adapted from the American College of Obstetricians and Gynecologists, *Exercise during pregnancy and the postpartum period.* Technical Bulletin No. 189, Feb. 1994.

---

in exercise with the intensity and frequency you did before becoming pregnant. In addition, intense physical activity results in changes that can be hazardous to your unborn baby and increase your risk of preterm birth. The American College of Obstetricians and Gynecologists has issued contraindications to exercising during pregnancy, as well as guidelines regarding exercising during pregnancy; these are given in the boxes on this page and 112 (112, 113). The contraindications to exercise during pregnancy include: pregnancy-induced hypertension (a pregnancy complication of high blood pressure); premature rupture of the membranes; preterm labor during a prior pregnancy and/or the current pregnancy; incompetent cervix with or without surgical treatment; second or third trimester bleeding;

The American College of Obstetricians and Gynecologists Guidelines for Exercise During Pregnancy*

1. Women who do not have any additional risk factors may continue to exercise during pregnancy. Regular exercise, at least three times per week, is preferable to intermittent activity.

2. Women should avoid exercise in the supine position (lying flat on your back) after the first trimester. Prolonged periods of motionless standing should also be avoided.

3. Women should be aware that during pregnancy they have less oxygen available for aerobic exercises. Women should modify the intensity of their exercise according to their symptoms (i.e., shortness of breath, lightheadedness). *Stop* exercising when fatigued and *do not* exercise to exhaustion.

4. Women should use judgment regarding exercise that could result in loss of balance, particularly during the third trimester of pregnancy.

5. Women who exercise during pregnancy should be particularly careful to eat an adequate diet.

6. Women who exercise during the first trimester of pregnancy should take additional steps to promote heat loss, including adequate hydration, appropriate clothing, and optimal environmental surroundings during exercise.

7. Because many of the physiologic changes of pregnancy persist four to six weeks after delivery, women should gradually resume their prepregnancy exercise regimens, depending on their physical capabilities.

* Adapted from the American College of Obstetricians and Gynecologists, *Exercise during pregnancy and the postpartum period*. Technical Bulletin No. 189, Feb. 1994.

or intrauterine growth retardation. Most of these factors have been discussed before as nonmodifiable risk factors for prematurity.

During pregnancy you will experience major cardiovascular changes, including increases in blood volume, the forcefulness of your heartbeat, and resting pulse. These changes are further exaggerated by your body position. For example, by the third trimester, you'll get the best blood flow to and from your heart when you are in a *left recumbent* position, that is, lying down on your left side. After the first trimester, the *supine position* (lying flat on your back) causes a relative obstruction of the blood return by the enlarged uterus. Such obstruction may even result in symptoms of supine hypotension, very low blood pressure (see Figure 14). As discussed in Chapters 3 and 4, *standing* is associated with an even greater obstruction of blood return than lying in the supine position (114–116).

During pregnancy you will also experience *respiratory changes,* which can reduce your ability to exercise. Because of an increase in resting oxygen requirements and the increased work of breathing resulting from the physical effects of the enlarged uterus on your diaphragm, there is less oxygen available for aerobic exercise during pregnancy. Pregnancy also results in *mechanical changes,* with a shift in your center of gravity caused by the growing uterus and enlargement of the breasts. This shift may make balance more difficult, affecting your ability to safely perform exercises that require balance (e.g., aerobics, dancing, riding a bike) (see Figure 15).

Pregnancy is associated with increases in basal metabolic rate and heat production; your unborn baby's

Figure 14

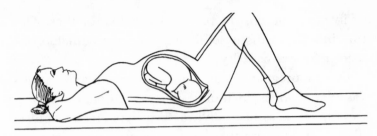

How lying flat on your back compresses the aorta.

temperature is about 1.5 degrees Fahrenheit greater than your body temperature. Moderate aerobic exercise causes additional increases in body temperature. Animal studies have shown that maternal temperature 2.25° Fahrenheit or more above normal during early pregnancy interferes with normal fetal development (117). This may explain the increased incidence of congenital anomalies among infants whose mothers used hot tubs and saunas during early pregnancy (117,118). The increase in blood volume that occurs after the first trimester helps to dissipate this additional body heat, which is why this risk is greatest only during early pregnancy.

Exercises that increase intra-abdominal pressure should be avoided during pregnancy because they increase your risk for premature uterine contractions (see Chapter 3, pp. 51–53). These exercises include the leg press (see Figure 16), weightlifting, squat thrusts, or any other exercise where you must bear down.

As most women who exercise regularly know, nutrition is important part of getting and staying fit. Pregnancy alone increases your caloric requirements by at least 300 calories per day during the third trimester;

Figure 15

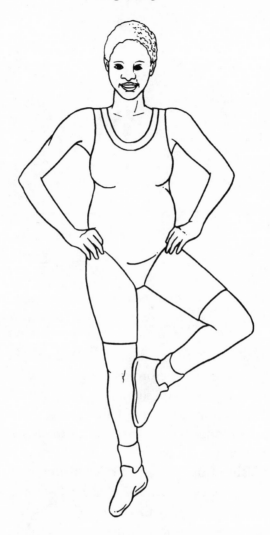

Balance is more difficult in later pregnancy.

exercise adds additional needs on top of that. Studies of infants of women who exercised intensely during pregnancy report a reduction in average birthweight of 300 to 500 grams (10 to 16 ounces) (119,120). One

Figure 16

Exercises such as leg presses increase intra-abdominal pressure.

study reported that, compared to women who stopped endurance exercise before 28 weeks' gestation, women who continued throughout pregnancy averaged 10 pounds lower weight gain, delivered eight days earlier, and had infants who were about one pound lighter (120). This reduction in birthweight may in part be due to a shunting of blood from the uterus to the muscles during exercise (121,122), as well as an inadequate caloric intake to cover the needs of pregnancy and intense exercise. During pregnancy you need to eat more frequently to maintain your blood sugar level; exercise reduces your blood sugar level even quicker (123). Therefore, if you plan to exercise while pregnant, you should plan your diet with extra care, making sure to include sufficient calories and frequent, small meals that are high in carbohydrates.

Figure 17

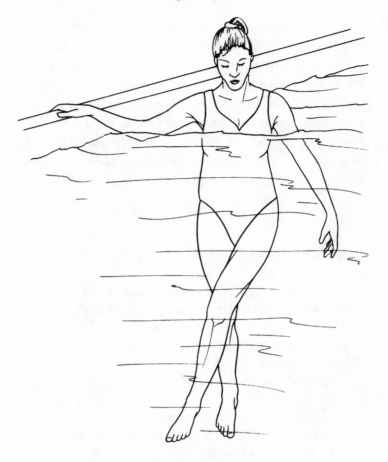

Swimming, a non-weight-bearing exercise.

Most women who performed regular weight-bearing exercise before pregnancy notice a progressive decline in their performance beginning during the first trimester (124). In one study of runners, aerobic dancers, and cross-country skiers, six out of ten women reported significantly decreased exercise performance in early pregnancy, and five out of ten had voluntarily stopped exercise completely by the third trimester

(125). Only one in ten women reported being able to maintain her level of performance at or near prepregnancy levels throughout pregnancy (120). In another study of well-conditioned runners, overall performance decreased by about 10 percent during the first trimester, gradually declining to about 50 percent of prepregnancy levels by the third trimester (126). Women who participate in non-weight-bearing exercise (i.e., cycling, swimming; see Figure 17) experience less of a decline in performance as pregnancy progresses (125,127,128).

> Marla, a thirty-four-year-old assistant editor and mother of twin teenagers, was 12 weeks pregnant. Marla takes an aerobic class three times a week, during her lunch hour, at a local health club. Although she had no other risk factors, Marla decided to change from aerobic classes during her lunch hours to swimming during the evening. She changed from aerobic exercise to swimming because it would be safer during pregnancy, and changed her workout time to evening because it would be less hectic. Marla also sought out the help of a nutritionist to plan a diet sufficient to cover the needs of pregnancy and exercise.

Remember, like most things in life (particularly when you are pregnant), use your judgment and do everything in moderation! It's not worth jeopardizing your pregnancy to set new personal fitness goals now, nor is it wise to risk your health by returning to your prepregnancy routine too quickly after delivery. Discuss your exercise program with your health-care professional so that he or she is aware of your level of activity and can help you make changes that are best for your health and that of your unborn baby.

Keep reminding yourself that you're making a short-term investment in the lifelong health of your child. I recommend you change the intensity, duration, and frequency of your exercise regimen during pregnancy. It's preferable to switch to less intensive types of exercise: changing from running to walking, cycling to swimming, aerobics to yoga. Cut down from a prepregnancy routine of one hour a day, five days a week to a pregnant routine of thirty minutes a day three times a week. Slow down and don't exercise to exhaustion or until you are perspiring heavily. Remember, when you exercise, you shunt blood away from the placenta and unborn baby to your muscles and increase your risk of low birthweight and prematurity. Is it really worth that price?

Of course, if you feel contractions while you're exercising, stop immediately, lie down, and follow the procedure I recommend on page ooo. Check with your doctor to see if it's safe for you to continue your exercise plan.

The risk factors presented in this chapter cover your choices both at work and at home, factors that may be a part of your daily or weekly habits, like drinking coffee or smoking cigarettes. Pregnancy lasts about nine months, and your baby is made only once. If ever there was a good time to take a hard look at your life and the factors that affect your health (and the health of your baby), it's now! Remember to check your risk factors on Checklist 3 on page 120, and include them in your total assessment in Chapter 7.

Checklist 3. Lifestyle Risk Factors

RISK FACTOR	Nonmodifiable	Modifiable	Modified
Alcohol intake			
Smoking habit			
Caffeine intake (more than 300 mg/day)			
Medications and drugs			
Recreational exercise			

6

Nutrition: You (and Your
Baby) Are What You Eat

NUTRITION PLAYS a major role during pregnancy, influencing your baby's birthweight as well as length of gestation. Some of these risks have already been mentioned in previous chapters, such as low weight gain and anemia. Unlike many other factors influencing your pregnancy, diet and nutrition are *completely under your control!* Remember: You (and your baby) are what you eat!

This chapter is divided into five sections. The first section reviews nonmodifiable factors present before this pregnancy. The second section presents factors in your current pregnancy, including some that are modifiable and some that are not. The third section discusses prenatal nutrition and the importance of a balanced diet. The fourth section discusses the latest research on the role of individual nutrients in preventing prematurity, and the fifth section includes a discussion of vitamin and mineral supplements and makes specific recommendations according to your risks.

How's Your Body Image?

For many women, the worst part about pregnancy is gaining weight, losing their waistlines, looking at themselves in the mirror as their body image changes week by week. Many husbands are not helpful in this process, either, with comments about how "fat" their wives have become. You may have worked very hard to attain the figure you had before you conceived and want to do the least amount of "damage" to it during pregnancy!

In contemporary American culture, we tend to uphold a very slender, youthful ideal. Body fat is something to be dieted, exercised, or liposuctioned away! We feel guilty when we have a second helping at mealtimes, say yes to an occasional dessert, or indulge in a frozen yogurt after dinner. Most of us are on a constant vigil against eating what we know is "bad" (but delicious!) and the daily weigh-in has long been as essential to our morning routine as brushing our teeth.

Pregnancy calls for a reevaluation of these ingrained concepts about diet and body image. The ability to conceive and maintain a pregnancy, as well as to carry that pregnancy to term is intrinsically tied to our nutritional state and how well we eat. Women do not begin to ovulate until their bodies are mature enough to sustain a pregnancy, which means attaining a minimum amount of body fat. Women with very low body weight or body fat will stop menstruating—Mother Nature thinks this person barely has enough caloric reserves for herself, and will not risk burdening her with the metabolic demands of a growing baby. Body fat and your weight before conception are your nutritional "insurance policies" for being able to get pregnant, and appropriate weight gain during pregnancy is the single most important step you can take toward assuring your baby a healthy birthweight! Appropriate weight gain during pregnancy will also increase your chances of successfully breast-feeding, if you choose this method of feeding your baby.

In this chapter I will discuss the various nutritional risk factors that can influence your pregnancy and the health of your baby. Keep in mind that as an adult, no matter how much you gain during pregnancy, if you return to your prepregnancy eating habits after giving birth, your weight will center back to your prepregnancy level within a few months, sooner if you are nursing. This will not happen, though, if you continue to eat as if you were still pregnant. Pregnancy is a state of health, but it causes major physiologic adjustments in every system of your body. These adaptations assure maximum efficiency in utilizing nutrients from your diet and help create the environment most conducive to your unborn baby's growth and health. Your metabolism changes during pregnancy, and those premenstrual "munchies" you experienced once a month before this pregnancy continue and even increase. Mother Nature wants that unborn baby to have a steady food supply, and as a result, the hormones of pregnancy will give you a good appetite!

Factors Present Before This Pregnancy

Although you can not change being *petite* (less than five feet tall), having *low body fat,* or being *underweight* before conception, these nonmodifiable factors are important for you to consider when assessing your total risk. To determine your percentage of body fat, use Figure 18. Find your height along the right-hand axis and your hip measurement (taken at the widest point) along the left-hand axis. Now, using a ruler or sheet of paper, align the straight edge to "connect" both measurements and read where it intersects the axis in the middle, your estimated percentage of body fat. The ideal range for adult women is between 22 and 28 percent; below about 18 percent is frequently associated with irregular periods and ovulation, and difficulty becoming pregnant (2). If you are already pregnant, low-percent body fat is a nonmodifiable risk, but if you are trying to become pregnant, it is one risk that's still modifiable.

Anna, a twenty-three-year-old professional ballerina, had been married for three years and had been unable to become pregnant. She and her husband had tried everything, and they were planning to see an infertility specialist. Her neighbor, a nutritionist, suggested that she try to gain some weight and reduce her dancing schedule. Anna was ready to try anything, so she took her neighbor's advice, cut down her dancing to three

Figure 18. Determining Percentage of Body Fat

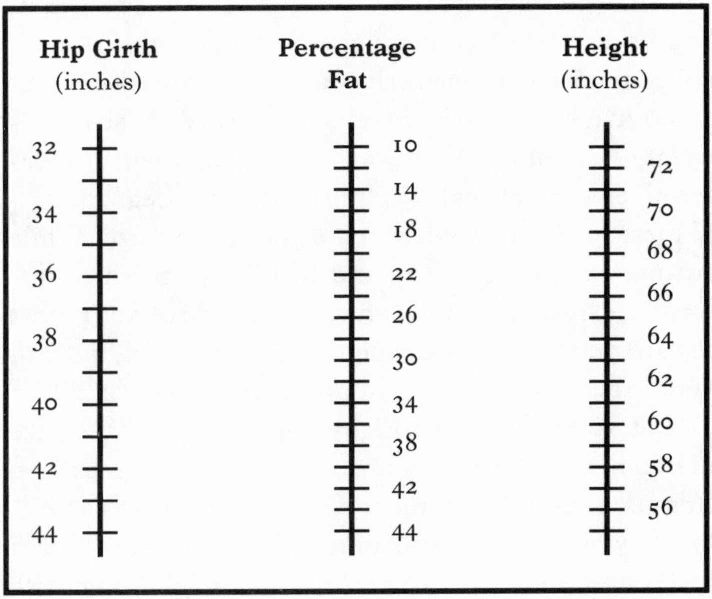

Hip Girth (inches)	Percentage Fat	Height (inches)
32	10	
	14	72
34	18	70
		68
36	22	66
	26	
38	30	64
		62
40	34	60
	38	
42	42	58
		56
44	44	

days a week, and changed to a higher-calorie, balanced diet. Within three months, Anna had gained 12 pounds, increasing her percent body fat from 17 percent to 20 percent, and her next pregnancy test was positive!

The next risk factor for you to evaluate is your weight-for-height, a percentage that determines whether you are underweight, overweight, or normal weight for your height and frame size. Ideally, your weight should be within a normal range for your height (90 to 119 percent) when you become pregnant. Research has shown that the rate of prematurity decreases as the mother's pregnancy weight increases (3–6). For example, one study reported prematurity rates of 114,

94, and 88 per 1,000 live births, respectively, for women who were less than 80 percent, 81 to 90 percent, and 90 to 110 percent weight-for-height (5). Another study reported prematurity rates of 158 and 115 per 1,000 live births, respectively, for normal versus over-weight women (6). Your weight-for-height will also de-termine your optimal weight gain during pregnancy.

First, you need to determine your frame size. While sitting, extend your arm and bend your forearm up-ward at a 90-degree angle; turn the inside of your wrist toward your body. Place the thumb and index finger of your other hand on the two prominent bones on either side of your elbow (see Figure 19). Measure the space between your fingers against a ruler or tape measure. Compare this measurement with the ranges in Table 6. Next, you need to determine your weight-for-height for your frame size. If you have a small frame, use Table 7; for a medium frame, Table 8; and for a large frame, Table 9. Find your height (without shoes) in the left-hand column, and follow across that line until you find your weight. The column header above your weight indicates whether you are underweight, normal weight, or overweight for your height.

Other nonmodifiable risk factors include recent diet-ing for weight reduction and recovery from a major ill-ness or surgery. Most weight-reduction diets limit your intake of meats and dairy products, rich sources of B vi-tamins, iron, calcium, and other minerals. Although you may have lost weight, you have probably done so at the expense of your body's reserves of these important nu-trients—nutrients that are essential during pregnancy. If you have just finished a weight-reduction program, be sure to include a daily vitamin supplement with extra

Figure 19

Determining your frame size by measuring the elbow.

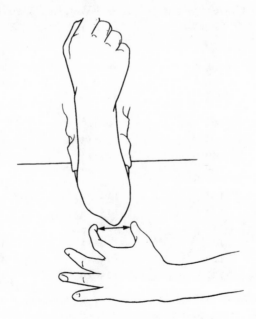

Table 6. Determining Your Frame Size by Your Elbow Breadth*

Height	Small Frame	Medium Frame	Large Frame
57"–62"	<2"	2¼"–2½"	>2⅝"
63"–70"	<2¼"	2⅜"–2⅝"	>2¾"

* Adapted from the 1971–75 *NHANES*.

Table 7.
Weight-for-Height Percentage, Small Frame*

Height	Underweight (≤ 90%)	Normal Weight (91–119%)	Overweight (≥ 120%)
57"	93	94–123	124
58"	94.5	95–125	126
59"	96	97–127	128
60"	98	99–130	131
61"	100	101–133	134
62"	103	104–137	138
63"	106	107–140	141
64"	108.5	109–144	145
65"	111	112–147	148
66"	114	115–151	152
67"	116.5	117–155	156
68"	119	120–158	159
69"	122	123–162	163
70"	124.5	125–165	166

* Adapted from the *Statistical Bulletin of the Metropolitan Life Insurance Company*, 1983; 64:2–9.

Table 8.
Weight-for-Height Percentage, Medium Frame*

Height	Underweight (≤ 90%)	Normal Weight (91–119%)	Overweight (≥ 120%)
57"	101	102–134	135
58"	102.5	103–136	137
59"	106	107–140	141
60"	107	108–142	143
61"	110	111–146	147
62"	113	114–149	150
63"	115	116–153	154
64"	118	119–156	157
65"	120.5	121–160	161
66"	123	124–164	165
67"	126	127–167	168
68"	129	130–171	172
69"	131.5	132–174	175
70"	134	135–178	179

* Adapted from the *Statistical Bulletin of the Metropolitan Life Insurance Company*, 1983; 64:2–9.

potency (but not megadoses; see the vitamin and mineral section of this chapter), and eat a balanced diet.

If you have recently had a major illness or are recovering from surgery, your nutritional status is probably not optimal. The stress of severe illness and surgery results in a loss of several nutrients, including vitamin C, protein, and the B vitamins. In addition, the immobility of being confined to bed results in a considerable loss of calcium from your bones! Document these nonmodifiable risks on your checklist, but make an extra effort to eat well during your pregnancy, and include

Table 9.
Weight-for-Height Percentage,
Large Frame*

Height	Underweight (≤ 90%)	Normal Weight (91–119%)	Overweight (≥ 120%)
57"	109	110–145	146
58"	112	113–148	149
59"	114	115–151	152
60"	116	117–154	155
61"	119	120–158	159
62"	122	123–162	163
63"	125	126–166	167
64"	129	130–171	172
65"	132	133–175	176
66"	135	136–179	180
67"	138	139–183	184
68"	141	142–187	188
69"	144	145–190	191
70"	146	147–194	195

* Adapted from the *Statistical Bulletin of the Metropolitan Life Insurance Company,* 1983; 64:2–9.

extra-potency vitamin and mineral supplements daily (but *not* megadoses; see the vitamin and mineral section of this chapter).

Factors Present During Your Current Pregnancy

Most of the changes that occur during pregnancy are in anticipation of your unborn baby's needs. Weight gain is a good example. Most women gain an additional

7 to 10 pounds of fat as part of their total weight gain during pregnancy as a sort of "nutritional insurance" provided by Mother Nature. Accumulation of this extra fat begins early in pregnancy, reaches a maximum during the second trimester (weeks 14 to 28), and is completely absent during the last trimester (weeks 29 to 40). This is opposite to the growth of your unborn baby, which is minimal during the first half of pregnancy and very rapid during the second half. Most of this extra fat is laid down over your back, abdomen, and upper thighs, which explains why clothes you wore comfortably before becoming pregnant may not fit even during the first trimester. This additional fat guarantees an adequate caloric reserve for both you and your baby during a time (the third trimester) when your diet may not be able to keep pace with the metabolic demands for yourself and your unborn baby. In addition, this extra fat helps ensure successful breast-feeding after delivery.

Many studies have shown a strong relationship between gestational weight gain and prematurity, as well as poor fetal growth (7–12). Inadequate weight gain, particularly during the first half of pregnancy, has been shown to be a risk for preterm birth in both singleton (10,11) and twin pregnancies (13,14). Among preterm births, higher weight gain is associated with better birthweights, with the incidence of very low birthweight (less than 3 pounds 4 ounces, or 1,500 grams) dropping from 25 per 100 births to about 5 per 100 births with maternal weight gain increasing from less than 16 pounds to more than 30 pounds. The incidence of low birthweight (less than 5 pounds 8 ounces, or 2,500 grams) among preterm births also fell from one in three births to one in four births across this range of maternal weight gain.

In 1990 the Institute of Medicine of the National Research Council published a report on nutrition during pregnancy by a panel of experts (1). This report made many recommendations, among them guidelines for weight gain during pregnancy depending on the woman's prepregnancy weight (weight-for-height before conception). For women who were *underweight* before conception (less than 90 percent weight-for-height), the recommended pattern of gain is about 5 pounds during the first trimester (first 13 weeks), and about a pound a week thereafter, for a total weight gain of 28 to 40 pounds. For *normal weight* women (90 to 119 percent weight-for-height), the recommended gain is 3.5 pounds the first trimester, followed by about a pound a week for the second and third trimesters, for a total gain of about 25 to 35 pounds. For *overweight* women (more than 120 percent weight-for-height), the recommended gain is about 2 pounds the first trimester and about ²/₃ of a pound per week for the second and third trimesters, for a total of 15 to 25 pounds. These recommendations, as well as normal ranges, are given in Figures 20, 21, and 22, respectively, for underweight, normal weight, and overweight women. Using these figures, plot your gain and weight changes as your pregnancy progresses, trying to stay within the recommended range on your weight-for-height weight gain grid. Bring this record to your obstetrician or health-care provider every visit to help him or her assess your weight gain progress. If you are pregnant with twins, your recommended weight gain grid is shown in Figure 23.

A common nutrition-related problem many women

Figure 20.

Weight Gain Grid for Underweight Women

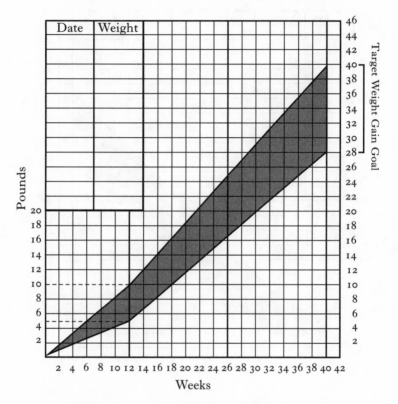

experience during pregnancy is nausea and vomiting. Often referred to as "morning sickness," as many as one-half to two-thirds of all pregnant women experience waves of nausea, that can occur in the morning or any time of the day. Most common in first pregnancies, morning sickness usually begins about six weeks after the start of the last menstrual period. Thought to occur as a result of rising hormone levels early in pregnancy, it usually disappears within several weeks, although

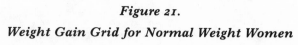

Figure 21.

Weight Gain Grid for Normal Weight Women

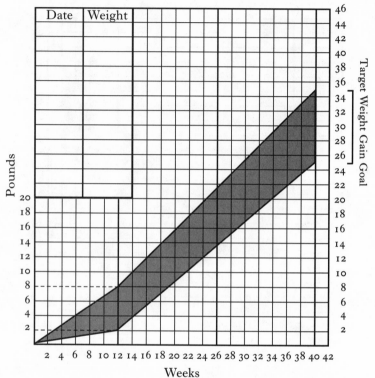

medical treatment may be necessary if the symptoms are severe and weight and fluid loss result. The traditional treatment is to eat small, frequent meals low in fat and high in carbohydrates, like dry crackers, before getting out of bed in the morning. Other suggestions include eating dry cereal, melba toast, vanilla wafers, or popcorn. Avoid taking beverages or soups during your meals, and have your partner or another family member cook if the odor of food triggers your nausea. Like many other things, what makes one woman sick may be

Figure 22.

Weight Gain Grid for Overweight Women

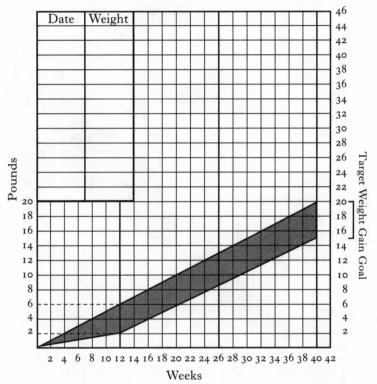

soothing to another. The most common offenders include coffee, garlic, fried foods, fish, meats, and onions. Some women find foods that are salty or tart, like potato chips or lemonade, helpful when they are nauseated. Trial and error will be your best guide, but if the nausea persists call your doctor.

Fasting, or going without food for prolonged periods, has been associated with the onset of labor (15, 16). When the blood sugar level drops as a result of fasting (hypoglycemia), the body compensates by releasing free

Figure 23.
Weight Gain Grid for Women
Pregnant with Twins

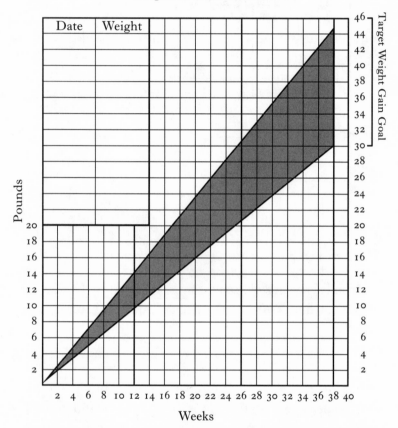

fatty acids from adipose tissue. One type of free fatty acid, arachidonic acid, is a precursor of prostaglandin, which stimulates uterine contractions. Hypoglycemia also causes a release of the catecholamine stress hormones, which also lead to uterine contractions. It is particularly important therefore that during pregnancy you eat frequently (every two to three hours), and include

breads, fruits, or rice or pasta (all of which contain carbohydrates) at each meal.

Iron-deficiency anemia, the most common nutritional disorder and the most important cause of anemia
in the world, is associated with a 2.5-fold increased risk
of prematurity and nearly a 3-fold increased risk of low
birthweight (17–20). During your initial prenatal visit,
your doctor probably tested your *hemoglobin* and *hematocrit,* the iron-containing components of your blood.
Many women have low iron stores, caused most often
by heavy monthly menstrual periods. Other causes of
low iron stores can include dieting, especially when
meats are excluded, bleeding ulcers or hemorrhoids,
and the frequent use of iron-binding medications, such
as antacids. Tea and coffee can also contribute to the
development of iron deficiency by inhibiting iron absorption from foods by as much as 40 percent for coffee
and as much as 65 percent for tea (21,22).

Iron is the single nutrient most likely to be lacking in
women's diets. It is absorbed in the gastrointestinal
tract only when needed, thereby preventing its excessive accumulation. The human body recycles the iron
in hemoglobin at about 90 percent efficiency, or, in
other words, it saves the iron in nine out of ten red
blood cells to be used again. For this reason, most men
have no problem maintaining a positive iron balance,
but most women do. Every month during the childbearing years, women lose iron in the menstrual blood
of their monthly periods. If menstrual bleeding is
heavy or prolonged, negative iron balance may result.
Most women have little or no iron stores because of
this monthly loss. When their stores of iron become
depleted, iron-deficiency anemia develops. The symp-

toms include lack of energy (because inadequate amounts of oxygen are being delivered to the tissues), dizziness, rapid heartbeat, and pallor. This same type of anemia frequently develops during pregnancy, but the cause of the iron drain is the developing baby rather than the monthly periods. The Centers for Disease Control and Prevention define iron-deficiency anemia during pregnancy as hemoglobin less than 11.0 g/dL (grams per deciliter) or hematocrit less than 33 percent in the first or third trimester, and hemoglobin less than 10.5 g/dL or hematocrit less than 31.5 percent in the second trimester (21).

Because most of the unborn baby's iron is acquired during the last trimester of pregnancy, premature birth also results in iron deficiency in the newborn. Women who gave birth before 32 weeks' gestation were more than twice as likely to have iron-deficiency anemia, and their newborns were almost 6.5 times more likely; those who gave birth before 37 weeks' gestation were more than 1.5 times as likely to have iron-deficiency anemia, and their newborns nearly 3 times more likely.

In the United States, the incidence of iron-deficiency anemia varies by maternal race and trimester of pregnancy. The Pregnancy Nutrition Surveillance System of the Centers for Disease Control and Prevention reported that among low-income women who gave birth in 1990, the incidence of anemia was 9.8 percent, 13.8 percent, and 33.0 percent, respectively, during the first, second, and third trimesters (22). The incidence by trimester was 6.1 percent, 9.3 percent, and 24.6 percent for white women, compared to 16.9 percent, 21.4 percent, and 45.8 percent for black women.

When iron stores become depleted, the absorption of

iron from the gastrointestinal tract becomes more efficient in an attempt to obtain more iron from the foods in the daily diet. As a rule, *heme iron,* the iron present in hemoglobin, is better absorbed than *nonheme iron,* iron from other sources, including iron-fortified cereals and breads and iron supplements. Heme iron includes the iron present in meat, fish, and poultry, which the human body actually recycles nearly as efficiently as it does from its own red blood cells. (Pregnancy is not a time to worry about cholesterol—this substance is actually one of the ingredients in the hormones needed during pregnancy!) Nonheme iron is absorbed much less efficiently, ranging from 5 to 10 percent. The absorption of nonheme iron can be enhanced by eating foods containing vitamin C (ascorbic acid) or fructose (fruit sugar) at the same meal. Foods rich in vitamin C include all citrus fruits, strawberries, red and green peppers, and tomatoes. Excessive amounts of fiber at the same meal can inhibit the absorption of nonheme iron. As I mentioned, coffee and tea can also reduce nonheme iron absorption by as much as 40 percent and 60 percent, respectively (23, 24). The absorption of heme iron, though, is not affected by other components of the diet. Heme-rich dietary sources of iron are given in Table 10.

The Recommended Dietary Allowances (RDAs) for iron double during pregnancy, from 15 milligrams to 30 milligrams. For women who can not meet these levels through diet alone, the Institute of Medicine recommends the routine use of 30 milligrams of ferrous iron per day beginning at about the twelfth week of gestation (1). The iron supplement should include a type of iron that is readily absorbed (ferrous fumarate

Table 10.

Heme-rich Dietary Sources of Iron

	Per 100 grams (3½ oz)	Per 100 calories
Pork sausage	9.3	2.6
Chicken liver	8.5	5.7
Oysters	6.7	3.3
Beef liver	6.2	2.9
Clams	4.1	4.1
Pot roast	3.4	1.1
Beef tenderloin	3.4	1.4
Shortribs	3.4	1.1
Sirloin steak	3.3	1.6
Sardines	3.1	1.5
Ground round beef	3.0	1.1
Duck	2.7	1.3
Turkey (dark meat)	2.4	1.3
Lamb chops	2.0	0.9
Shrimp	1.6	1.4
Ocean perch	1.4	0.6
Turkey (white meat)	1.3	0.8
Fried chicken	1.3	0.5
Ham	1.1	0.6
Roasted chicken	1.0	0.6
Veal cutlet	0.9	0.4
Canadian bacon	0.9	0.5
Tuna (solid white)	0.7	0.4

or ferrous sulfate), be free from additional ingredients that could interfere with absorption (such as calcium, magnesium, or zinc)(25–28), and, if part of a multivitamin, not contain excessive levels of additional vitamins or minerals. The best iron absorption is from supplements composed of ferrous sulfate, ferrous ascorbate, ferrous fumarate, or ferrous citrate; poor absorption occurs with iron supplements made of ferrous phosphate or ferrous carbonate.

If your health professional suggests that you take an iron supplement, I recommend Feosol Capsules or Tablets (SmithKline Beecham), Ferro-Sequels (Lederle Labs), or Slow Fe Tablets (CIBA Consumer). For an iron supplement with added vitamin C, I recommend either Niferex Vitamin C (Central Pharmaceuticals) or Irospan Tablets (Fielding Company). It is not possible to overdose on the iron in foods, but it is a real possibility with iron supplements. Every year there are about two thousand cases of iron poisoning, mainly among young children who have taken iron supplements intended for adults. A lethal dose of ferrous sulfate for a two-year-old child is about 3 grams; for an adult, it's about 10 grams. Make sure to keep your iron supplements out of reach of children, and only take them as prescribed by your health professional.

Prenatal Nutrition and the Importance of a Balanced Diet

Nutrition is the process by which your body uses food. During pregnancy, nutrition is of vital importance because the food you eat influences your health and the health of your unborn baby. When nutritionists or dietitians speak about nutrition, they are referring to the six groups of essential nutrients found in foods: proteins, carbohydrates, fats, vitamins, minerals, and water.

Proteins are made up of amino acids, structural units that are essential in building and repairing tissue, as well as the formation of blood, bones, and the brain. They are also vital components of enzymes, substances that regulate body processes; hormones; and antibodies, part of your immune system. You need more protein during pregnancy to build the placenta, for increases in your breasts, blood, uterus, and, of course, for the growth of the baby. Some of the amino acids in protein cannot be made by the body (essential amino acids) and must be included in the diet. For this reason, the quality of the protein you eat during pregnancy is important. Protein foods that contain all essential amino acids (complete proteins) include meat, fish, poultry, and dairy products (milk, cheese, eggs). Be careful to avoid uncooked meats or poultry, as they may be a source of parasites or bacterial food poisoning. If you are a vegetarian, you must be especially careful about combining foods to make sure you get all the essential amino acids in your meals. Combinations that assure this include cereal and milk, macaroni and cheese, peanut butter and whole-grain bread, and rice and beans. During pregnancy, protein needs increase about 20 percent, to about 60 grams. The protein content of some common foods is given in Table 11.

Carbohydrates provide the primary energy source for adults, and the only energy source that can be used for your unborn baby's developing nervous system. Sometimes called sugars, carbohydrates come in two forms: simple and complex. Simple sugars are found in fruits, honey, milk, and refined sugar. Complex sugars include potatoes, corn, wheat, and rice. Fiber, a nondigestible

Table 11.

Protein Content of Common Foods

Food	Amount	Protein (grams)
Complete Proteins		
Frankfurter	1¾ oz	7
Hamburger	4 oz	22
Porterhouse steak	8 oz	25
Rib roast	8 oz	28
Veal cutlet	3½ oz	33
Veal loin chop	3½ oz	23
Lamb loin chop	3½ oz	23
Ham	3½ oz	33
Pork loin chop	3½ oz	29
Chicken	3½ oz	29
Turkey	3½ oz	25
Halibut	3 oz	23
Tuna	3 oz	25
Milk	8 oz	8
Cottage cheese	8 oz	30
Egg	1 large	6
Cheddar cheese	2 oz	15
Yogurt	8 oz	12
Incomplete Proteins		
Tofu bean curd	½ cup	10
Split pea soup	1 cup	10
Peanut butter	2 tbsp	8
Pasta, cooked	1 cup	5
Oatmeal	1 cup	5
Rice	1 cup	4
Bread	1 slice	2
Dry cereal	1 cup	2

source of carbohydrate, absorbs water as it passes through the digestive system and helps with bowel function. High-fiber foods include bran and whole-grain cereals, apples, dried fruits, and raw vegetables. Carbohydrate needs double during pregnancy, to about 200 grams per day. As discussed earlier, fasting, which results in hypoglycemia (low blood sugar), is dangerous during pregnancy because it can lead to premature contractions and premature birth. Include carbohydrate-containing foods like fruits and fruit juices, milk and milk products, and breads, grains, and pasta in your meals and snacks during pregnancy to prevent hypoglycemia and to meet your and your baby's energy needs. The carbohydrate content of some common foods is given in Table 12.

Fat is the most concentrated source of energy in our diets. When you do not get enough calories in your diet from carbohydrates, the body uses fat for energy (either from the diet or from adipose tissue), and one of the by-products of its breakdown (ketones) may be toxic to your unborn baby. Some components of fat are essential, such as linoleic acid, and must be supplied by the diet. Two servings a day of butter or oil will meet this need. Fat should supply about 30 percent of your total daily calories, which is about 2,200 calories during the first trimester and about 2,500 calories during the second and third trimesters. Since fat supplies about 9 calories per gram, you should have about 73 grams of fat in your diet during the first trimester and about 83 grams thereafter. Table 13 gives the fat content of some common foods.

Vitamins and minerals are essential nutrients that function as either cofactors in various metabolic processes or in the body's structure. Unlike proteins, carbohy-

Table 12.
Carbohydrate Content of Common Foods

Food	Amount	Carbohydrate (milligrams)
Breads		
Cracked wheat	1 slice	12
White enriched	1 slice	12
Whole wheat	1 slice	11
Danish pastry	1 small	16
Sugar doughnut	1 average	22
Grains and pasta		
Oatmeal	1 cup	26
White rice	¾ cup	23
Corn grits	1 cup	27
Pasta, cooked	1 cup	44
Fruits (all raw)		
Cantaloupe	¼ melon	8
Peach	1 medium	10
Pear	½ medium	15
Orange	1 medium	18
Figs	2 large	20
Apple	1 medium	22
Banana	1 small	22
Vegetables (cooked)		
Broccoli	1 stalk	5
Winter squash	½ cup	15
Peas	½ cup	18
Lentils	⅔ cup	19
Kidney beans	⅔ cup	21
Sweet corn	1 medium ear	22
Baked potato	1 medium	32
Dairy		
Milk (skim or whole)	8 oz	12
Cottage cheese	3½ oz	3
Ice cream	1/6 qt.	19

Table 13.
Fat Content of Common Foods

Food	Amount	Fat (grams)
Hamburger	3½ oz	19
Ice cream (16 percent fat)	6 oz	18
Mixed nuts	1 oz	15
Avocado	½ medium	15
Vegetable oils	1 tbsp	14
French fries	3 oz	13
Butter	1 tbsp	12
Margarine	1 tbsp	11
Mayonnaise	1 tbsp	11
Ice cream (10 percent fat)	6 oz	11
Cream cheese	2 tbsp	10
Bacon	3 strips	9
Whole milk	8 oz	9
Ham	3 oz	9
Cheese	1 oz	8
Tuna, oil-packed	3 oz	7
Egg, boiled	1 large	6
Milk, 2 percent fat	8 oz	5
Tuna, water-packed	3 oz	1
Skim milk	8 oz	0

drates, or fats, vitamins do not contribute calories but rather function in converting carbohydrates into energy, proteins into healing or growing tissue, and fats into storage for energy use at a later time. They are only needed in small amounts, although during pregnancy the requirements for nearly all vitamins and minerals increase (see Table 14). When taken in large amounts, vitamins can actually do more harm than good, including interfering with the metabolism of other vitamins and even causing birth defects. For ex-

Table 14. Summary of the RDAs for Nonpregnant and Pregnant Women and Food Sources of Nutrients

Nutrient	Nonpregnant	Pregnant	% Increase	Dietary Sources
Folic acid	180 mg	400 mg	+122	Leafy vegetables, liver
Vitamin D	200 IU	400 IU	+100	Fortified dairy products
Iron	15 mg	30 mg	+100	Meats, eggs, grains
Calcium	800 mg	1,200 mg	+50	Dairy products
Phosphorus	800 mg	1,200 mg	+50	Meats
Vitamin B_6	1.6 mg	2.2 mg	+38	Meats, liver, enriched grains
Vitamin B_1	1.1 mg	1.5 mg	+36	Enriched grains, pork
Zinc	12 mg	15 mg	+25	Meats, seafood, eggs
Vitamin E	8 mg	10 mg	+25	Vegetable oils
Vitamin B_2	1.3 mg	1.6 mg	+23	Meats, liver, enriched grains
Protein	50 mg	60 mg	+20	Meats, eggs, dairy, legumes
Selenium	55 μg	65 μg	+18	Seafood, kidney, liver
Iodine	150 mcg	175 mcg	+17	Iodized salt, seafood
Vitamin C	60 mg	70 mg	+17	Citrus fruits, tomatoes
Energy	2,200 kcal	2,500 kcal	+14	Proteins, fats, carbohydrates
Magnesium	280 mg	320 mg	+14	Seafood, legumes, grains
Niacin	15 mg	17 mg	+13	Meats, nuts, legumes
Vitamin B_{12}	2.0 mcg	2.2 mcg	+10	Animal proteins
Vitamin A	800 μg	800 μg	no increase	Dark green, yellow vegetables
Vitamin K	8 mg	10 mg	no increase	Green leafy vegetables

ample, large doses of vitamin C interfere with the body's ability to use vitamin B_{12}; large amounts of vitamin B_6 interfere with the body's ability to use vitamin B_2; and both vitamins D and E are antagonistic to vitamin A. Congenital malformations have resulted from maternal intake of 40,000 to 50,000 IU of vitamin A, about fifteen times the recommended intake during pregnancy, and 4,000 IU of vitamin D, about ten times the recommended intake. Vitamin deficiency is rare in this country because most commonly used foods are either fortified or enriched, including the addition of vitamins A and D to milk, B vitamins and iron to breakfast cereals and breads, and iodine to table salt.

The two most important minerals in the diet are iron and calcium. Iron has already been discussed. Calcium, another essential nutrient that must be supplied from your diet, is important for bone and tooth development. Dairy products are the most concentrated source of calcium in our diets, and contribute complete protein as well. If milk gives you gastrointestinal problems (bloating, gas, cramps), the culprit is probably the type of sugar found uniquely in milk—lactose. Lactose must be broken down by the body before it can be absorbed during digestion. Many women lack the enzyme necessary to break down lactose, and therefore find it difficult to drink milk. I recommend that you try LactAid brand milk or Dairy Ease brand milk, which have been processed to break down the lactose. LactAid brand milk also comes calcium-fortified, providing 500 milligrams per eight-ounce glass, so two and a half glasses provide you with all your daily calcium needs. Yogurt and cheese are also great sources of calcium; these and other sources are listed in Table 15.

Table 15.
Calcium Content of Common Foods

Food	Amount (oz)	Calcium (mg)
Milk		
Calcium-fortified skim	8	500
Skim or whole	8	266
Cheese		
Cottage, uncreamed	4	28
Cottage, plain creamed	4	68
Cream cheese	2	40
Cottage cheese, lowfat	4	100
American	2	364
Cheddar	2	386
Swiss	2	522
Yogurt		
Fruited	8	300
Flavored	8	335
Plain	8	360
Low-fat frozen	3	112
Ice Cream		
Vanilla (12% fat)	4	164
Ice Milk		
Vanilla	4	156

Water is a substance vital to life, second in importance only to oxygen. Like many people, you may not consider water an important part of your diet, but it certainly is! Water plays an important role in regulating body temperature through the evaporation of moisture from the skin and lungs. The loss of 1 to 2 percent of total body water triggers thirst, the loss of 10 percent constitutes a serious health hazard, and a 20 percent loss can result in death. During pregnancy you should be drinking at least six to eight glasses of water a day. This amount is important to help prevent kidney infections, as well as to prevent dehydration, another possible cause of premature uterine contractions.

The foundations for the prenatal diet in the United States are the Recommended Dietary Allowances (RDAs), mentioned in the discussion about iron (29). These recommendations, formulated by the Food and Nutrition Board of the National Research Council, are revised periodically (most recently in 1989), and specify levels of selected nutrients by gender, age, and for pregnancy and lactation. A summary of the RDAs for nonpregnant and pregnant women and dietary sources of recommended nutrients are given in Table 14. Contrary to popular belief, the requirements for all nutrients do not double during pregnancy. Only the requirements for iron, folic acid, and vitamin D increase by 100 percent or more over nonpregnant levels, while other nutrients such as calcium, phosphorus, thiamine, and pyridoxine increase by 33 to 50 percent. Protein, zinc, and riboflavin increase about 20 to 25 percent, whereas energy, selenium, magnesium, iodine, niacin, and vitamins A, B$_{12}$, and C increase by 18 percent or less. The RDAs for pregnancy have been translated into two weeks of menus for fall and winter (Table 16) and two weeks of menus for spring and summer (Table 17). The caloric content of these diets can be varied by increasing or decreasing the portion sizes, but the balance of food choices provides all the RDAs during pregnancy.

New Research on Individual Nutrients

Research indicates that several specific nutrients may play important roles in preventing prematurity. For example, recent studies have shown a significant reduction in prematurity with the intake of 2 grams (2,000 milligrams) of elemental *calcium* as calcium carbonate per day (30–33). The same effect could probably be achieved with 2 grams of calcium from dairy sources. It is believed that the calcium acts on reducing the contractibility of the smooth muscle of the uterus. Calcium in supplements and in foods may also lower prematurity indirectly by reducing the incidence of preeclampsia, a hypertensive complication of pregnancy (31–33). Supplementation with magnesium, another nutrient that may also act on smooth muscle, has also been shown to reduce the incidence of premature birth (34).

In 1938 and 1939, studies in London found halibut liver oil to be effective in reducing prematurity (35); recent studies have confirmed these findings from more than fifty years ago, demonstrating the positive effect of long-chain *omega-3 fatty acids* in reducing prematurity (36–39). Fish are high in this substance, as well as fish liver oils. It is believed that long-chain omega-3 fatty acids act through inhibiting the synthesis of prostaglandin, a substance that initiates preterm labor.

Whenever possible, include fish in your diet during pregnancy, but check with your local health authority to make sure the fish sold in your area is free from contaminants; follow their advice in selecting fresh, unpolluted fish, and avoid raw fish, such as sushi.

Table 16. Sample Menus for Fall/Winter

Breakfast	Lunch	Snack	Dinner	Snack
Waffles** and syrup Milk* Orange juice	Tuna melt on whole wheat** Vegetable soup	Oatmeal cookies Milk*	Meatloaf Mashed potatoes Peas and carrots	Angel food cake Hot tea
Pancakes** and syrup Sausage links Apple juice	Beef chili Crackers** Fresh grapes	Fig Newton cookies Milk*	Steak Roasted potatoes Spinach soufflé	Bread pudding Hot tea

Hot oatmeal**
Steamed milk*
Grapefruit juice
	Grilled cheese
	  with bacon
	Lentil soup
		Raisin bagel
		Farmer cheese
			Spaghetti and
			  meatballs
			Garlic bread
			Caesar salad
				Gingerbread
				Warm milk*

French toast** Sausage patties Sliced oranges	Franks and beans Cornbread** Applesauce	Graham crackers** Cheddar cheese	Beef stew Sweet potatoes Green Peas	Datenut bread Warm milk*

Hot Cream
  of Wheat**
Cheese cubes
Tomato juice

New England
  clam chowder

Raisin toast**
Milk*

Roasted turkey
Stuffing
Cranberry sauce

Pumpkin pie
Hot cider

Cream of Rice**
Bacon strips
Rye toast**

Oyster stew
Cheese toast**
Sliced pears

Gingersnaps
Milk*

Roast beef
Baked squash
Green beans

Baked apple
Hot tea

Hot grits**
Raisin toast**
Apple slices

Cream of
  tomato soup
Bacon, lettuce and
  tomato on
  toasted wheat**

Graham crackers**
Fruit yogurt*

Baked ham
Scalloped potatoes
Carrots

Baked custard*
Hot chocolate*

* Milk and milk products should be enriched with extra calcium and be skim, low-fat, or whole depending on recommended weight gain.

** Breads and cereals should be enriched with B vitamins and iron.

Table 17. Sample Menus for Spring/Summer

Breakfast	Lunch	Snack	Dinner	Snack
Whole-grain cereal* Milk* Banana	Grilled chicken Sliced tomatoes Potato salad	Frozen yogurt	Baked fish Macaroni and cheese Broccoli	Strawberries and milk*
Wheat germ Fruit yogurt* Blueberries	Tuna salad Coleslaw Fresh grapes	Frozen yogurt	Cheese pizza Tossed salad	Frozen yogurt
Whole wheat toast** Cottage cheese* Orange juice	Shrimp salad on whole wheat** Fresh plums	Cheese and crackers**	Grilled hamburger on whole wheat bun* Tomatoes and onions	Blueberries and milk*
Toasted bagel** Farmer cheese* Cantaloupe	Egg salad on rye** Fresh nectarines	Vanilla Wafers Custard	Fried chicken Salad	Strawberry ice cream

Cheese omelet	Chef salad	Ice cream sandwich	Grilled salmon	Bananas
Sliced peaches	Potato salad		Summer squash	with milk**
	Fresh peaches		Spinach salad	
Toasted English	Cottage cheese	Pudding	Beef salad with	Ice cream sundae
muffin**	Pineapple slices	Oreo cookies	asparagus and	
Sliced cheese	Whole wheat		broccoli	
Honeydew melon	crackers**			
Scrambled eggs	Pasta salad	Lemon wafers	Shish kebab	Fruit yogurt*
Shredded cheese	Roast beef	Milk*	Tomatoes and	
Strawberries	Sliced watermelon		peppers	
			Roasted potatoes	

* Milk and milk products should be enriched with extra calcium and be skim, low-fat, or whole depending on recommended weight gain.

** Breads and cereals should be enriched with B vitamins and iron.

Zinc is another nutrient shown to be associated with an increased risk of prematurity. In one recent study, women whose diets contained 40 percent or less of the RDA for zinc had a 2-fold increased risk of low birthweight and nearly a 3.5-fold increase of preterm delivery (40). When iron-deficiency anemia was also present, low dietary zinc intake was associated with more than a 5-fold increased risk of very preterm birth (less than 33 weeks). Zinc and iron in supplements or multivitamins should not be taken together, as they impair each other's absorption (25–28).

Vitamin and Mineral Supplements

If you eat a balanced diet, vitamin and mineral supplements are not really necessary. Because of busy schedules, hectic lifestyles, and many other perfectly good reasons, however, many women do not eat a balanced diet every day. During pregnancy, this affects not just you but your baby as well, so you may want to consider a supplement. Vitamin supplements should not contain excessive amounts of vitamins (less than twice the level of the RDA) and should not contain iron or other minerals. My favorite vitamin supplement is One-A-Day Essential (Miles, Inc.). If you have been dieting for weight reduction or been recovering from a major illness or surgery before pregnancy, I suggest using Sigtab Tablets or Zymacaps (Roberts Pharmaceuticals) or Stresstabs Advanced (Lederle Labs) because of their higher potency. The supplement should be taken with food, at mealtime. Recently, the Centers for Disease Control issued a recommendation that all women of childbearing age consume 0.4 milligrams of folic acid per day from at least one month prior to becoming pregnant through the first three months of pregnancy, for the purpose of reducing specific birth defects (41). If you are planning a pregnancy, improving your nutritional status is a very positive step, including making sure you get an adequate amount of folic acid. Taking a daily vitamin supplement before pregnancy is a healthy way to get ready for pregnancy.

If you decide to take a calcium supplement, check what kind of calcium it contains. For example, calcium carbonate provides the most concentrated source of elemental calcium, followed by calcium citrate, calcium lactate, and calcium gluconate. Calcium carbonate supplements, though, may have more side effects, such as constipation, gas, and bloating. All calcium supplements inhibit iron absorption and therefore should not be taken with iron supplements or with food containing iron. Calcium supplements made from calcium chelates (gluconate, lactate, or amino acids) or refined calcium contain substantially lower levels of lead and other pollutants compared to supplements made from dolomite, bonemeal, or "natural" sources, such as oyster shells (42).

Avoid high-priced calcium supplements, which are typically sold in health food stores. If you have a history of kidney stones, check with your physician before taking any calcium supplement.

Assessing Your Nutritional Risks

Now that we've finished your nutritional assessment, look over your checklist. Although you cannot change how tall you are or how much you weighed before becoming pregnant, you do have complete control over your diet, and therefore how much you gain and how fast. When making food choices, whether it's at home or when eating out, think in terms of "nutrient density": How much nutrition are you getting for the calories you're spending? A quarter-pounder with cheese provides a lot of nutrition—heme iron, B vitamins, protein, and calcium—but turn down the French fries, which are mostly fat and empty calories. Occasional sweets are fine, but think nutrition—snacks of cheese, fruits, milk or milkshakes are much better for you and your growing baby! Plot your weight gain, and try to maintain a good pattern throughout your pregnancy, particularly during the first half. Use Checklist 4 at the end of this chapter to rate your nutritional risks, and include them in your overall rating in Chapter 7.

Checklist 4. Nutritional Risk Factors

	Nonmodifiable	Modifiable	Modified
HISTORIC RISK FACTORS			
Petite (<5'o")			
Low body fat (<18%)			
Underweight (≤90% weight-for-height)			
Recent dieting for weight reduction			
Recovery from illness/surgery			
CURRENT RISK FACTORS			
Inadequate early gain (<20 weeks)			
Inadequate late gain (>20 weeks)			
Fasting			
Iron-deficiency anemia			
Inadequate iron intake			
Inadequate calcium intake			

7

*Adding Up Your Total Risk
and Planning a Course
of Action*

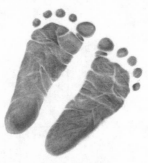

N OW THAT you have evaluated all of your personal risks and made all the changes that you could,
let's again take that test that appeared at the end of
Chapter 1 on page 19. Compare the number of *modifiable* risk factors you identified in your original test with
the number of *modifiable* and *modified* risk factors
you've identified in your retest, the checklist at the end
of this chapter. I hope you'll find that you've been able
to reduce your risk for premature birth. Even small
changes can add up to make a big difference in the outcome of your pregnancy! I hope these changes also improve the overall quality of your life. I believe that,

pregnant or not, you deserve the benefit of a life that has more rest and less noise and stress!

I'm recapping the suggestions and recommendations made in the previous chapters here to help you review your own situation and to encourage you to custom-tailor my advice according to your special needs. Keep in mind, the more *nonmodifiable* risk factors you've identified, the more important it is for you to reduce or eliminate your *modifiable* risk factors! Bring this master checklist with you when you visit your doctor to help him or her evaluate and monitor your overall risk.

Make sure your doctor is aware of all of your risk factors for prematurity, including ones he or she may not have thought to ask you about. Your doctor may not ask you whether you have elderly relatives or preschoolers at home, but please don't hesitate to call these factors to his or her attention. If your profile in-cludes a lot of nonmodifiable risk factors, ask your doc-tor to work even more closely with you to make sure you're eating right, getting enough rest, and doing whatever else you can to create a healthier environment for you and your baby.

Ask your doctor to review with you how to recognize uterine contractions and what to do if and when they occur. Uterine contractions may be perceived as a heaviness in the abdomen or as pain in the mid- to lower back, accompanied by a tightening of the uterus. When you feel this heaviness or pain, you should place your hands on your abdomen, at the top of the uterus, to determine if these sensations are accompanied by a tightening or hardening of the uterus. It is important for you to:

1. Recognize that uterine contractions are occurring;
2. Identify what activities bring on contractions; and
3. Stop that activity and sit down or preferably, lie down on your left side, until the contractions subside.
4. Drink at least a glass or two of water, since dehydration can also cause uterine contractions.
5. Call your doctor immediately and report your contractions. Follow his or her advice.

Review with your doctor your "game plan of action" if you go into labor. Remember, you are a critical member of your own health-care team.

When you get back home, take another close look at the things you take for granted—for example, how much you stand, how often you go up and down stairs—and make changes wherever you can. Walk through your house and evaluate how you can become more organized. Take steps to reduce clutter in your home, which, in turn, will reduce the amount of housework (and physical effort) in your daily life. Make an effort to decrease the amount of stair climbing, lifting, carrying, standing, and driving you do. Turn over the vacuuming to someone else! Lower the volume on the TV and stereo, and cut down on your exposure to noise in other ways if you can. If possible, get help from friends and relatives with food shopping, chores, babysitting, and carpooling. Remember, stress and physical effort can be as prevalent in your home life as in your work life.

Try to modify your work commute (reducing the amount of standing and driving, if possible). When you're on the job, make a conscious effort to sit as often as possible. Cut down on the physical efforts you make—lifting, carrying, and so on—if you can. Avoid noise and fatigue as much as you can, and try to fit in at least two rest periods during the day. Ask your employer to help you modify your work environment to reduce the number of hours you work, or devise a compromise between working at home and at the office.

Remember that lifestyle changes are completely under your control. Stop smoking and drinking. Don't take any drug—not even a vitamin or an aspirin—without checking with your doctor. Reduce your caffeine intake to fewer than 300 milligrams per day. Follow medical guidelines regarding recreational exercise. You'll soon be able to get back in shape after the birth; don't push yourself to exercise vigorously now.

Eating right is so important now. To figure out your particular needs, start by determining your frame size and weight-for-height percent (see pages 128–30), then establishing your ideal weight gain pattern and target weight gain goal. Make sure you're getting enough iron and calcium, from foods or supplements, and choosing the best vitamin supplement for your needs. Remember, we are what we eat, and that goes for your unborn baby, too!

There are many things that we do not know about prematurity. Sadly, prematurity cannot be completely prevented. However, identifying and modifying your personal risk factors are the best ways to improve your chances of having a healthy, full-term pregnancy.

Your Personal Risk Assessment Questionnaire

Answer each question below as yes (1 point) or no (0 point) in either column A or B, as indicated.

	Col. A	Col. B

Family Background

1. Do you consider yourself African-American? — yes no (Col. A)
2. Were you born in the United States? — yes no (Col. A)
3. Are you younger than eighteen or older than thirty-five? — yes no (Col. A)
4. Is your annual household income less than $8,000 for a family of two, or less than $10,000 for a family of three? — yes no (Col. A)
5. Are you a single parent? — yes no (Col. A)
6. Do you have preschool children at home? — yes no (Col. A)
7. Do you have more than two children at home? — yes no (Col. A)
8. Do one or more elderly relatives live with you? — yes no (Col. A)

Gynecological, Obstetrical, and Medical History Factors

Before this pregnancy, have you had

9. —any spontaneous abortions? — yes no (Col. A)
10. —any induced abortions? — yes no (Col. A)
11. —any preterm births? — yes no (Col. A)

Were any of your previous newborns

12. —born dead (stillborn)? — yes no (Col. A)
13. —less than 5¼ pounds at birth? — yes no (Col. A)
14. —dead within one month after birth? — yes no (Col. A)
15. Do you have a history of infertility treatments? — yes no (Col. A)

		Col.		*Col.*	
		A		*B*	
16.	Did your mother take diethylstilbestrol (DES) when she was pregnant with you?	yes	no		
17.	Is this your first pregnancy?	yes	no		
18.	Have you given birth four or more times before?	yes	no		
19.	Did you have any preexisting medical conditions?	yes	no		

Current Obstetrical Factors

20.	Have you had any vaginal bleeding after twelve weeks?	yes	no		
21.	Do you have any placental complications?	yes	no		
22.	Have you been told you have an incompetent cervix?	yes	no		
23.	Do you have premature rupture of the membranes (PROM)?	yes	no		
24.	Have you had one or more vaginal infections?	yes	no		
25.	Are you pregnant with more than one baby (multiple gestation)?	yes	no		

Home and Work Environment Factors

26.	Do you climb stairs at home?			yes	no
27.	Do you do much lifting at home?			yes	no
28.	Do you do much carrying at home?			yes	no
29.	Do you do much standing at home?			yes	no
30.	Is your home environment noisy?			yes	no
31.	Do you spend much time driving (carpool, groceries, errands)?			yes	no
32.	Is your job high-stress or physically demanding?			yes	no
33.	Do you stand while commuting to and from work?			yes	no
34.	Do you stand most of the time at work?			yes	no

	Col. A		Col. B
35. Do you do much lifting at work?		yes	no
36. Does your job require much physical exertion?		yes	no
37. Do you have irregular work hours?		yes	no
38. Does your job involve shift work?		yes	no
39. Do you work more than eight hours per day?		yes	no
40. Do you work more than forty hours per week?		yes	no
41. Do you become fatigued at work?		yes	no
42. Is your work environment noisy?		yes	no
43. Are you under a lot of stress at work?		yes	no
44. Do you drive at work or commute to work?		yes	no

Lifestyle Factors

	Col. A		Col. B
45. Do you drink alcohol?		yes	no
46. Do you smoke cigarettes?		yes	no
47. Do you drink more than two cups of coffee per day?		yes	no
If you participate in recreational exercise,			
48. —do you exercise on your back or until fatigued?		yes	no
49. —do you exercise until you perspire?		yes	no

Nutritional Historical Factors

	Col. A		Col. B
50. Are you shorter than five feet tall?	yes	no	
51. Can you pinch less than one inch of fat on your arm?	yes	no	
52. Are you underweight for your height?	yes	no	
53. Have you recently been dieting to lose weight?	yes	no	
54. Have you recently had a major illness or surgery?	yes	no	

	Col. A	Col. B

Nutritional Factors in the Current Pregnancy

Have you been told that you have

55. —to eat more frequently (don't fast)	yes	no
56. —not gained enough weight before 20 weeks?	yes	no
57. —not gained enough weight after 20 weeks	yes	no
58. —iron-deficiency anemia?	yes	no
59. —an inadequate iron intake?	yes	no
60. —an inadequate calcium intake?	yes	no

8

The U.S. Laws on Work and Pregnancy

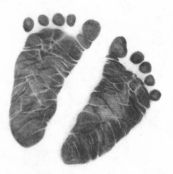

OVER THE PAST two hundred years a variety of laws and policies on work and pregnancy have been enacted, including some from the League of Nations, labor unions, and other organizations. Many were put into practice during World War II, when women were essential to the workforce. Many countries have what is called an "enlightened maternity policy," which includes specified periods of leave, cash benefits, and job protection; the amount of leave and cash benefits varies from country to country. In this chapter I'll compare the present-day work and pregnancy laws in a number of countries.

Comparison with European Maternity Laws

Maternity leave is such a widely accepted concept throughout the world that prior to 1993, when the United States established the Family Leave Act, America was the only industrialized country that lacked any national legislation regarding maternity benefits and rights. Maternity leaves date back as far as 1878 in Germany, 1928 in France, and 1937 in Denmark, Finland, and Sweden. Although countries vary in their specific provisions, all European plans contain three basic elements: entitlement to a specified period of time away from work before and after childbirth, cash benefits payable during the leave period, and protection of job rights. As shown in Figure 24, many industrialized countries around the world have a high proportion of women in their labor forces, ranging from more than 30 percent in Italy to nearly 65 percent in Sweden.

An international comparison of antepartum (before childbirth) and postpartum (after childbirth) maternity leave is shown in Figure 25. Antepartum leave ranges from four to twelve weeks, and postpartum leave ranges from five to twenty-six weeks. Maternity leave policies reflect an interest in the well-being of mothers and infants as well as an effort to encourage women both to have more children and to remain in the labor force (1).

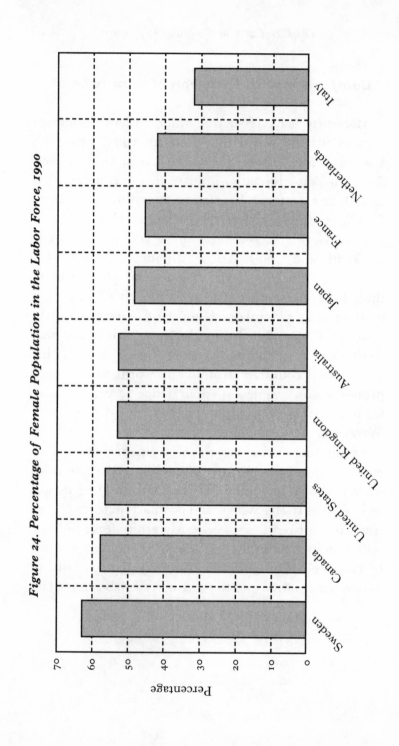

Figure 24. Percentage of Female Population in the Labor Force, 1990

Figure 25. International Comparison of Maternity Leave

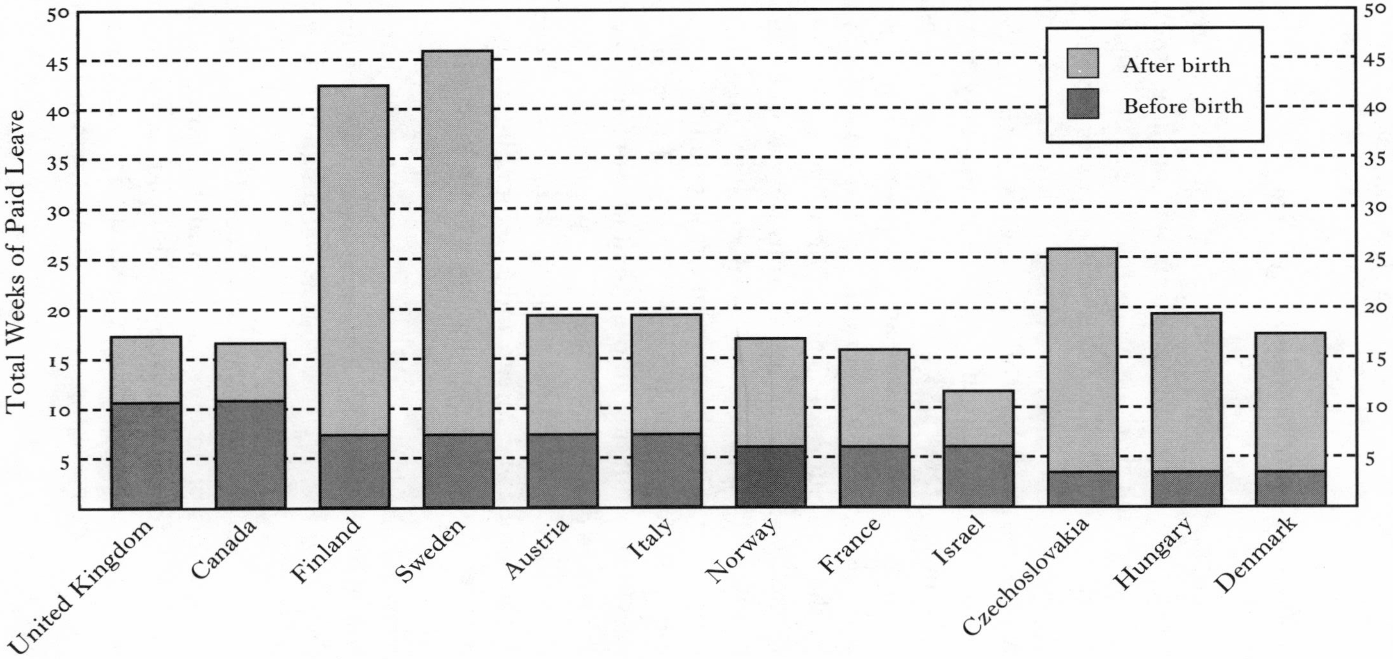

History of U.S. Maternity Laws

The first statewide law in the United States for working women was passed in Wisconsin in 1867, restricting their working hours to no more than ten hours per day and sixty hours per week. It was generally believed that standing, stretching, and repetitive motions would weaken the childbearing potential of young women and should therefore be limited. By 1900 sixteen other states also had passed laws restricting the number of hours a woman could work. The first federal ruling regarding women was handed down in 1908 by the U.S. Supreme Court. This ruling stipulated that women should be excused from long working hours, particularly if the work involved standing. By 1912 thirty-four states had passed legislation limiting working hours for women; between 1910 and 1920, six states passed laws limiting employment of women at the time they were due to give birth. The prevailing philosophy during the 1920s and 1930s was that women belonged in the home to bear, rear, and care for children, and that married women who worked were taking jobs away from men and single women. Working women who were not fired when they got married often left work voluntarily when they became pregnant, knowing that they would be fired as soon as the pregnancy began to show.

The workforce shortage of World War II forced a change this philosophy, as 4.5 million women entered the labor force. The Women's Bureau, in conjunction with the Children's Bureau, issued "Standards for Maternity Care and Employment of Mothers in Industry" in July 1942. These standards recommended that a pregnant working woman give first consideration to her own health and the health of her unborn child, and recommended opportunities for prenatal care, a workday limited to eight daytime hours, rest periods, and six weeks' prenatal leave and two months' postnatal leave. The standards also recommended work restrictions, including no lifting, continuous standing, or exposure to toxic substances. Paid maternity leave was not part of the recommendations.

The first federal legislation in the United States was passed in 1946 as an amendment to the Federal Railroad Unemployment Insurance Act (2). Pregnant employees were entitled to temporary disability insurance and received weekly cash and sickness benefits for maternity. Financed by employee contributions and payroll tax, the act allowed a maximum of sixteen and one-half weeks of leave.

During the 1950s through the 1970s, mandatory unpaid leave was the norm for most pregnant employees. Under the best conditions, this meant that the woman could be reinstated in the same or a comparable job. Most of the time, however, reinstatement was at a lower level, with lower pay, and with loss of benefits and seniority. This was eventually outlawed when, in 1978, the Pregnancy Disability Amendment to Title VII of the Civil Rights Act of 1964 was passed (PL 95-555). This amendment stipulated that pregnancy discrimination was a form of sex discrimination, and that both were illegal. This law provided that pregnancy-related disabilities should be treated the same as any other disability.

Current Pregnancy Laws in the United States

The two most important current federal laws concerning pregnancy are the Pregnancy Discrimination Act of 1978 and the Family and Medical Leave Act of 1993. The Pregnancy Discrimination Act requires companies with fifteen or more employees to treat pregnancy the same as any other temporary disability. This act prohibits firing a woman simply because she is pregnant, and if a company has a disability policy, pregnant women receive the same income and/or medical benefits granted to any other temporarily disabled employee. This act does not require employers to guarantee a pregnant employee's position while she is on leave; rather it requires employers to guarantee job security to pregnant women if, and to the same extent that, they guarantee job security to other people returning from other disability leaves. Likewise, the act requires employers to provide disability insurance for pregnancy if, and to the same extent that, they provide disability insurance for other conditions. This means that a pregnant woman can get a leave for the period of time prescribed by her physician for the "disability" of pregnancy and childbirth, usually four to six weeks after a vaginal delivery and six to eight weeks after delivery by cesarean section.

Depending on your modifiable and nonmodifiable risks, as summarized in your checklist in Chapter 7, your physician may recommend work leave to prevent prematurity, and he or she can prescribe pregnancy disability leave under this act. Discuss your work, home, and family situations, and other risks for prematurity with your doctor so that you can plan a compromise that best benefits your situation and optimizes your chances of a healthy pregnancy.

Passed by Congress twice, and vetoed by President Bush twice (in 1990 and 1991), the Family and Medical Leave Act was finally enacted on February 5, 1993, and became effective on August 5, 1993. This federal law requires employers with fifty or more employees to provide workers with up to twelve weeks of *unpaid leave* a year for the birth or adoption of a child, foster care of a child, illness of a spouse, child, or parent, or because of an employee's own illness. This new act does not decrease an employer's obligations under any collective bargaining agreement or employee benefit plan providing greater employee family leave rights. It also does not prohibit an employer from formulating a more generous plan; nor does it supersede any state or local law that provides greater employee family leave rights.

Both male as well as female employees are entitled to leave under this law, although because it is *unpaid leave,* many people cannot afford the loss of salary, particularly when they are expecting a baby. Your employer must maintain your health insurance coverage, and although you do not lose seniority or benefits, your employer is not required to allow your benefits to accrue further during the leave.

Under this law, you need to give your employer thirty days' notice that you intend to take a leave, if at all possible. If you go into premature labor or have complications requiring you to stop working, you should notify your employer as soon as possible. Your employer may require you to substitute categories of paid leave for part of the twelve-week unpaid period. For example, your employer can decide not to let you take paid vacation and sick time *in addition* to the twelve weeks' unpaid leave. You may be limited to twelve weeks total leave, even if you would like to add on additional time you have accrued to your guaranteed leave.

Before the passage of the Family Leave Act, most states already had laws in effect regarding pregnancy and work leave. Twenty-three states have laws that cover both private and state employees (persons working in the public sector). The duration of leave varies from sixteen hours to one year. Some states allow for a "reasonable period" of leave, while others do not specify the amount of leave permitted. The work leave is normally unpaid, although under some laws employees are entitled, or may be required, to use sick leave or other categories of paid leave, or a combination of paid and unpaid leave. Most states require that after such leave, the employee is entitled to job reinstatement to the original or equivalent position and to retain seniority and fringe benefits. Several states set requirements for eligibility for leave, which usually includes having worked for one year, full-time (thirty-five to forty hours per week), and without a break in service.

Five states (California, Hawaii, New Jersey, New York, Rhode Island) and Puerto Rico have *temporary disability insurance (TDI)* laws that provide partial salary replacements for nonwork-related disabilities, including childbirth and pregnancy-related conditions. TDI pays partial salaries to employees during the actual period of disability caused by pregnancy or childbirth on the same basis as other disabilities due to job-related accidents or illnesses. The percentage of salary paid to employees under TDI varies from 50 to 65 percent of an employee's weekly wages, and the duration of disability pay varies from twenty-six to fifty-two weeks. State maternity/family leave laws are usually administered by state human rights or civil rights commissions, and claims for TDI are usually filed with state departments of labor. A summary of benefits by state is given in Table 18, a summary of TDI laws is given in Table 19, and enforcement and/or administration sources by state is given in Table 20. I've listed some additional resources in the Bibliography.

Table 18. Summary of States with Parental, Family, or Medical Leave Legislation

State (effective date)	Employer Size (number of employees)	Employees Covered	Maximum Length of Leave (weeks)	Provision	Must Employer Continue to Contribute to Preexisting Health Benefits?	Job Guarantee	Comments
Alaska (Jan. 1, 1992)	> 21	All employees	18 (over 24 months for family leave/ over 12 months for pregnancy or child care leave)	Birth/adoption Family illness	Yes	Same or comparable position	
California (Jan. 1, 1992)	≥ 50 employees	All employees	16 (over 2 years)	Birth/adoption Family illness (includes spouse if over age 65) Foster care	No	Same or comparable position	
Connecticut (July 1, 1990)	≥ 75	All employees	16 for private; 24 for state employees (over 2 years)	Birth/adoption Family illness Personal illness	State employees—yes; employee contributes portion of premium that employer would have contributed had employee not taken leave. Private employees—no	Same or comparable position	

State (effective date)	Employer Size (number of employees)	Employees Covered	Maximum Length of Leave (weeks)	Provision	Must Employer Continue to Contribute to Preexisting Health Benefits?	Job Guarantee	Comments
Delaware (July 20, 1984)		State employees who are adoptive parents	6	Adoption	No explicit provision	No explicit provision	
District of Columbia (Oct. 3, 1990)	≥ 50; phase down to ≥ 20 in 1994	All employees	16 (over 2 years)	Birth/adoption/placement of foster child Family illness Personal illness	Yes—employer must maintain employee's health insurance under same conditions as if employee had not taken leave.	Same or comparable position	"Family care" includes anyone with whom employee maintains committed relationship.
Florida (Oct. 1, 1991)		State employees	24 (over 2 years)	Birth/adoption Family illness	No	Same or comparable position	

State (effective date)	Employer Size (number of employees)	Employees Covered	Maximum Length of Leave (weeks)	Provision	Must Employer Continue to Contribute to Preexisting Health Benefits?	Job Guarantee	Comments
Hawaii (July 1992)		State employees; private employees (≥ 100), begins in 1994	4 (over 2 years)	Birth/adoption Family illness	No	Same or comparable position	
Illinois (Sep. 1993)		Eligible state employees	52	Birth/adoption Family illness	No—employer must continue health insurance, but employee pays full premium.	Same or comparable position	"Family care" includes any member of employee's family or household.
Iowa (1988)	≥ 4	All female employees except for household, domestic	8	Pregnancy, childbirth, related medical conditions	No	No provision	This leave is to be used when employee has no other leave or has insufficient time under sick leave, temporary disability, or health plan.

State (effective date)	Employer Size (number of employees)	Employees Covered	Maximum Length of Leave (weeks)	Provision	Must Employer Continue to Contribute to Preexisting Health Benefits?	Job Guarantee	Comments
Kentucky (July 15, 1982)	≥ 1	Only adoptive parents	6	Adoption of child under age 7	No explicit provision	No explicit provision	
Louisiana (1987)	≥ 26	All female employees	16	Pregnancy, childbirth, related medical conditions	No	No provision	
Maine (Aug. 4, 1988)	≥ 25	All employees	10 (over 2 years)	Birth/adoption Family illness Personal illness	No	Same or comparable position	
Maryland (July 1, 1988)		All state employees in executive branch	12	Birth/adoption/ foster care Family illness	No	Same or comparable position	Leave is dependent on supervisor approval.
Massachusetts	≥ 6, except for nonprofit social clubs and fraternal associations	All female employees with 3 consecutive months of full-time employment with the same employer	8	Birth/adoption	Employer must provide same benefits as are provided to all other employees on leave of absence. Employer may also offer paid leave.	Same or comparable position	

State (effective date)	Employer Size (number of employees)	Employees Covered	Maximum Length of Leave (weeks)	Provision	Must Employer Continue to Contribute to Preexisting Health Benefits?	Job Guarantee	Comments
Minnesota (Aug. 1, 1987)	≥ 21	All employees	6	Birth/adoption SF 409 allows employees to use accrued sick days to care for sick child.	No—employer must continue to make insurance coverage available to employee, but can require employee to pay the entire premium.	Same or comparable position	SF 409 also allows employees 16 hours of unpaid leave each year to attend school conferences or classroom activities.
Montana	≥ 1, except fraternal, charitable, or religious nonprofit associations	Female employees in private sector	"Reasonable" leave of absence	Pregnancy	No	Same or comparable position	
New Jersey (May 1, 1990)	≥ 75; phase down to ≥ 50 in 1993	All employees	12 (over 2 years)	Birth/adoption Family illness	No	Same or comparable position	
North Dakota (Jan. 1, 1990)		All state employees	12 (for full-time workers) 8 (for part-time workers)	Birth/adoption/ foster care Family illness	No—employer must provide continued coverage, but is not required to pay costs of coverage.	Same or comparable position	

State (effective date)	Employer Size (number of employees)	Employees Covered	Maximum Length of Leave (weeks)	Provision	Must Employer Continue to Contribute to Preexisting Health Benefits?	Job Guarantee	Comments
Oklahoma (Aug. 25, 1989)		All state employees	Not explicit	Birth/adoption Family illness (for child or any dependent adult)	No—employee can continue state group insurance if she or he pays full premium	Same position	
Oregon (Parental leave: Jan. 1, 1988) (Family care leave: Jan. 1, 1992)	≥ 25 for parental leave ≥ 50 for family care leave (employee must work for 180 days before being eligible)	All employees	12 (over 2 years)	Birth/adoption Family illness	No	Same or comparable position	If at least one parent works for a covered employer, the two parents must split the 12 weeks granted by statute into nonconcurrent parts unless their employers agree to other terms.

State (effective date)	Employer Size (number of employees)	Employees Covered	Maximum Length of Leave (weeks)	Provision	Must Employer Continue to Contribute to Preexisting Health Benefits?	Job Guarantee	Comments
Rhode Island (July 1987)	≥ 50	All employees	13 (over 2 years)	Birth/adoption Family illness Personal illness	Yes—employer must maintain its contribution to employee's preexisting health benefits. However, before taking leave, employee must pay employer a sum equal to the premium required to maintain employee's health benefits. Employer will return this payment to employee within 10 days after returning to job.	Same or comparable position	
South Carolina (1986)		All state employees	5 days of accrued sick leave (over 2 years)	Family illness	No explicit provision	No explicit provision	

State (effective date)	Employer Size (number of employees)	Employees Covered	Maximum Length of Leave (weeks)	Provision	Must Employer Continue to Contribute to Preexisting Health Benefits?	Job Guarantee	Comments
Tennessee	≥ 100	All female employees with 12 consecutive months of full-time employment with the same employer	16	Pregnancy, childbirth, nursing of infant	Employer must continue to pay benefits only if they are provided to other employees on leaves of absence.	Same or comparable position, assuming proper notice had been given to employer	
Vermont	≥ 10	Female employees in the private sector with 12 consecutive months of employment at an average of 30 hours per week for the same employer	12	Pregnancy, childbirth	Yes—employer must continue to provide benefits, but may require employee to pay entire cost of benefits.	Same or comparable position	

State (effective date)	Employer Size (number of employees)	Employees Covered	Maximum Length of Leave (weeks)	Provision	Must Employer Continue to Contribute to Preexisting Health Benefits?	Job Guarantee	Comments
Washington (Sep. 1, 1989)	≥ 100	All employees	12 (over 2 years); employee's accrued sick leave may be used to care for sick child	Birth/adoption Child's illness	No	Same or comparable position	Employer may limit or deny leave to up to 10% of workforce that is designated as key personnel, or highest-paid 10% of its employees.
West Virginia (July 7, 1989)		All state employees	12	Birth/adoption Family illness	No—employer must continue group health insurance, but employee pays full premium.	Same or comparable position	

State (effective date)	Employer Size (number of employees)	Employees Covered	Maximum Length of Leave (weeks)	Provision	Must Employer Continue to Contribute to Preexisting Health Benefits?	Job Guarantee	Comments
Wisconsin (Apr. 25, 1988)	≥ 50	All employees	6 (parental); 2 (family care); 2 (personal medical); no more than 8 weeks over 1 year for a combination of reasons related to family and medical leave	Birth/adoption Family illness Personal illness	Yes—employer must maintain its contribution to employee's preexisting health benefits. If health insurance coverage is provided, the employer may require that the employee pay the full premium for 8 weeks of coverage into an interest-bearing escrow account.	Same or comparable position	

SOURCES: Center for Policy Alternatives, Women's Legal Defense Fund, and Families and Work Institute.

As of April 1993, some form of leave legislation was pending in nine states: Kansas, Massachusetts, Nevada, New York, North Carolina, Ohio, Pennsylvania, South Dakota, and Utah. Several states have employment policies for their own employees related to family leave, including: Arizona, Colorado, Kansas, Maryland, and New York.

The Massachusetts Employment Leave Insurance Bill is exemplary, as it would establish temporary disability insurance to provide income to workers on family and medical leave. This bill covers all employees for up to twenty-six weeks for personal medical leave or to care for a sick family member (defined as any "person living in the immediate household of the employee"); and covers employees for sixteen weeks of parental leave, which can be taken on a full- or part-time basis.

Table 19. Summary of Temporary Disability Insurance*

Jurisdiction	Employee Contribution	Employer Contribution	Amount of Benefits
California	1.25% of first $31,000 annual earnings	None	Minimum $50/week; maximum $336/week; based on schedule
Hawaii	½ premium cost; maximum $2.78/week	Balance of costs	58% average weekly wage; maximum set each year
New Jersey	0.5% of first $16,000 annual earnings; maximum $80.53/year	Varies according to claims experience	⅔ average weekly wage; maximum $304/week
New York	0.5% of earnings; maximum $0.60/week	Balance of costs	50% weekly wage; maximum $170/week
Puerto Rico	0.3% of first $9,000 annual earnings	Same	65% average weekly wage; minimum-maximum: $12–113/week
Rhode Island	1.3% first $38,000 annual earnings	None	4.2% total wages in one quarter; maximum $374, plus dependent allowance

* Adapted from U.S. Department of Labor, Office of the Secretary, Women's Bureau. *State Maternity-Family Leave Law.* Washington, D.C.: Government Printing Office, June 1993.

Table 20. Enforcement and/or Administration State Maternity/Family Leave Laws*

Note: Not all states have maternity/family leave laws. In those instances the federal law applies.

Alaska	State Department of Labor, P.O. Box 21149, Juneau, Ala. 99802-1149. Phone: (907) 269-4900.
California	Title 2, Part 2.8, Chapter 6, enforced by the Department of Fair Employment and Housing, 2000 O St., suite 120, Sacramento, Calif. 95814. Phone: (916) 445-9918. Title 2, Part 2.6, Chapter 2.5, administered by the Department of Personnel Administration, 1515 S St., North Building, suite 400, Sacramento, Calif. 95814. Phone: (916) 324-0455. Temporary disability insurance claims are filed with the Health and Welfare Agency, Employment Development Department, Disability Insurance Benefits Branch, 750 N St., Sacramento, Calif. 95814. Phone: (916) 654-8198 or (916) 739-2944 for recorded information.
Colorado	State Civil Rights Commission, 1560 Broadway, suite 1050, Denver, Colo. 80202. Phone: (303) 894-2997.
Connecticut	Title 31, Chapter 557, enforced by the State Department of Labor, 200 Folly Brook Blvd., Wetherfield, Conn. 06109. Phone: (203) 566-4550.

* Adapted from U.S. Department of Labor, Office of the Secretary, Women's Bureau. *State Maternity-Family Leave Laws*. Washington, D.C.: Government Printing Office, June 1993.

Title 5, Chapter 67, administered by the Department of Administrative Services, 165 Capitol Ave., Hartford, Conn. 06106. Phone: (203) 566-4720.

Title 46a, Chapter 814c, enforced by the Commission on Human Rights and Opportunities, 90 Washington St., Hartford, Conn. 06101. Phone: (203) 566-3350.

Delaware   State Personnel Commission, Townsend Building, P.O. Box 1401, Dover, Del. 19903. Phone: (302) 739-4195.

District of Columbia   Department of Human Rights and Minority Business Development, 2000 14th St., 3rd floor, Washington, D.C. 20009. Phone: (202) 939-8740.

Florida   Department of Management Services, 2737 Centerview Dr., Knight Building, suite 110, Koger Executive Center, Tallahassee, Fla. 32299-0950. Phone: (904) 488-2786.

Georgia   State Personnel Board, 200 Piedmont Ave., room 418W, Atlanta, Ga. 30334. Phone: (404) 656-2725.

Hawaii   State Department of Labor, Enforcement Division, Fair Employment Practices, 830 Punchbowl St., room 340, Honolulu, Hawaii 96812. Phone: (808) 586-8770.

Temporary disability insurance claims are filed with the State Department of Labor and Industrial Relations, Disability Compensation Division, P.O. Box 3769, 830 Punchbowl St., room 210, Honolulu, Hawaii 96812. Phone: (808) 586-9188.

Illinois	Office of Central Management, 519 Stratton Building, Springfield, Ill. 62706. Phone: (217) 782-7638.
Iowa	State Civil Rights Commission, 211 East Maple St., 2nd floor, Grimes State Office Building, Des Moines, Iowa 50319. Phone: (515) 281-4121 or (800) 457-4416.
Kansas	State Commission on Civil Rights, Landon Street Office Building, 8th floor, 9100 SW Jackson St., suite 851, South, Topeka, Kansas 66612. Phone: (913) 296-3206.
Kentucky	Kentucky Labor Cabinet, Division of Employment Standards and Mediation, 1049 U.S. 127 S., Frankfort, Ky. 40601. Phone: (502) 564-2784.
Louisiana	State Department of Labor, Commission on Human Rights, room 244, 1001 North 23rd St., P.O. Box 94094, Baton Rouge, La. 70804. Phone: (504) 342-3076.
Maine	Commission on Human Rights, State House Station #51, Augusta, Maine 04333. Phone: (207) 624-6050.
Maryland	State Department of Personnel, 301 West Preston St., Baltimore, Md. 21201. Phone: (410) 225-4847.
Massachusetts	Commission Against Discrimination, One Ashburton Place, Boston, Mass. 02108. Phone: (617) 727-3990.
Minnesota	Department of Human Rights, 500 Bremer Tower, Minnesota St. and 7th Pl., St. Paul, Minn. 55101. Phone: (612) 296-5665.

Missouri	Labor and Industrial Relations Commission, Commission on Human Rights, 3315 W. Truman Blvd., Jefferson City, Mo. 65109. Phone: (314) 751-3325.
Montana	Title 49, Chapter 2, Part 3, enforced by the Department of Labor and Industry, Human Rights Commission, 1236 6th Ave., Helena, Mont. 59624. Phone: (406) 444-2884.
New Hampshire	Commission for Human Rights, 163 Loudon Rd., Concord, N.H. 03301. Phone: (603) 271-2767.
New Jersey	Department of Law and Public Safety, Division on Civil Rights, 383 West State St., Trenton, N.J. 08625. Phone: (609) 292-4605.
	Temporary disability insurance claims are filed with the State Department of Labor, Division of Unemployment and Disability Insurance, CN058, 10th floor, John Fitch Plaza, Trenton, N.J. 08625. Phone: (609) 292-2460.
New York	Executive Department, Division of Human Rights, 55 W. 125th St., New York, N.Y. 10027. Phone: (212) 870-8400.
	Temporary disability insurance claims are filed with the State Workers' Compensation Board Disability Benefits Bureau, 100 Broadway-Menands, Albany, N.Y. 12241. Phone: (518) 474-6680.
North Dakota	State Department of Labor, 600 East Blvd., 6th floor, State Capitol, Bismarck, N.D. 58501. Phone: (701) 224-2660.

Oklahoma	Office of Personnel Management, Jim Thorpe Building, 210 N. Lincoln Blvd., Oklahoma City, Okla. 73150. Phone: (405) 521-2177.
Oregon	Bureau of Labor and Industries, Civil Rights Division, State Office Building, 1400 SW 5th Ave., Portland, Ore. 97201. Phone: (503) 229-5841 or (800) 452-7813.
Puerto Rico	Department of Labor and Human Resources, Anti-Discrimination Unit, 505 Muñoz Rivera Ave., Hato Rey, P.R. 00918. Phone: (809) 754-5292. Temporary disability insurance claims are filed with the Department of Labor and Human Resources, Bureau of Employment Security, Disability Insurance Program, 505 Muñoz Rivera Ave., Hato Rey,˜ P.R. 00918. Phone: (809) 754-2146 or 754-2147.
Rhode Island	State Department of Labor, Division of Labor Standards, 220 Elmwood Ave., Providence, R.I. 02907. Phone: (401) 457-1808. Temporary disability insurance claims are filed with the State Department of Labor, Temporary Disability Insurance Division, 101 Friendship St., Providence, R.I. 02903. Phone: (401) 277-3630
South Carolina	State Budget and Control Board, Division of Human Resource Management, 1201 Main St., suite 1000, AT&T Building, Columbia, S.C. 29201. Phone: (803) 737-0940.

Tennessee	Title 4, Chapter 21, Part 4, enforced by the Tennessee Human Rights Commission, Cornerstone Square Building, suite 400, 530 Church St., Nashville, Tenn. 37243. Phone: (615) 741-5825. Title 8, Chapter 50, Part 8, administered by Tennessee Department of Personnel, Employee Relations Division, 2d floor, James K. Polk Building, 505 Deaderick St., Nashville, Tenn. Phone: (615) 741-1646.
Texas	Classification Office, State Auditor's Office, P.O. Box 12067, Austin, Tex. 78711-2067. Phone: (512) 479-4880.
Vermont	Office of the Attorney General, 109 State St., Montpelier, Vt. 05609-1001. Phone: (802) 828-3171.
Virginia	Department of Personnel and Training, James Monroe Building, 101 N. 14th St., Richmond, Va. 23219. Phone: (804) 225-2314.
Washington	State Department of Labor and Industries, 925 Plum St. HC710, Olympia, Wash. 98504. Phone: (206) 753-3475.
West Virginia	Division of Labor, Wage and Hour Section, Capitol Complex, Building 3, Charleston, West Virginia 25305-0570. Phone: (304) 558-7890.
Wisconsin	Department of Industry, Labor and Human Relations, Equal Rights Division, P.O. Box 8928, Madison, Wis. 53708. Phone: (608) 266-6860.

Glossary

Abruptio placentae: a complication of pregnancy that occurs when the placenta separates from the uterus before labor.

Basal metabolic rate: the amount of energy (usually in calories) required in a resting state.

Catecholamines: hormones (epinephrine and norepinephrine) released during exercise, stress, emotional states, and physical activity.

Cervix: the mouth of the uterus, normally closed during pregnancy. *Incompetent cervix* refers to the complication during pregnancy that occurs when the cervix spontaneously opens, resulting in loss of the pregnancy if early in pregnancy, or prematurity if later in pregnancy.

Diethylstilbestrol (DES): a medication given to some pregnant women from the 1950s through the 1970s to prevent spontaneous abortion. It has been associated with congenital malformations of the uterus and vagina in daughters of women who took it during pregnancy.

Early preterm: pregnancy of 32 weeks' gestation or less.

Ectopic pregnancy: pregnancy that does not occur in the uterus; most commonly, when the embryo implants in a Fallopian tube.

Embryo: the product of conception, from the moment of fertilization to the end of the eighth week after fertilization.

Extremely low birthweight: infants with birthweights of 1,000 grams or less (2 pounds 3 ounces).

Fallopian tubes: the two ducts that transport the ovum from the ovary to the uterus.

Fecundity: the ability of a woman to become pregnant.

Fertility: the ability of a woman to give birth.

Fetal Alcohol Effects (FAE): partial expression of the syndrome produced when an infant has been exposed to alcohol before birth.

Fetal Alcohol Syndrome (FAS): full expression of the syndrome produced when an infant has been exposed to alcohol before birth. The syndrome includes: pre- and postnatal growth retardation, facial malformations, mental retardation, and other congenital malformations (cardiac, cleft palate).

Fetus: the term used to describe the unborn baby from the ninth week after fertilization to birth.

Hematocrit: the percentage of the whole blood volume occupied by the red cells after being centrifuged.

Heme iron: iron derived from hemoglobin.

Hemoglobin: the respiratory pigment of red blood cells, having the reversible property of taking up and releasing oxygen.

Hypertension: high blood pressure.

Induced abortion: intentional termination of a pregnancy by medical or mechanical means.

Interpregnancy interval: the time (in months) between the birth of a child and the next conception.

Intrauterine growth retardation (IUGR): birthweight below the 10th percentile for gestational age; also known as small-for-gestational age (SGA).

Iron-deficiency anemia: a condition in which the amount of iron in the blood is lower than normal; caused by blood loss, inadequate dietary intake, or poor absorption.

Large-for-gestational age (LGA): birthweight above the 90th percentile for gestational age.

Low Birthweight (LBW): birthweight less than 2,500 grams (5 pounds, 8 ounces).

Miscarriage: spontaneous loss of a pregnancy before 24 weeks' gestation.

Nativity: pertaining to place of birth (U.S.-born versus foreign-born).

Neonatal death: death of an infant within twenty-seven days after birth.

Normal weight: weight-for-height before pregnancy within 91 to 119 percent.

Overweight: weight-for-height before pregnancy of 120 percent or more.

Ovulation: release of the egg (ovum) from the ovary.

Placenta: the organ within the uterus that supplies the fetus with oxygen and nutrients; sometimes known as the afterbirth.

Placenta previa: a complication of pregnancy that occurs when the placenta lies over the cervix (the mouth of the uterus), resulting in hemorrhage before or during labor.

Premature rupture of membranes (PROM): opening of the amniotic membranes ("bag of waters") before birth.

Prematurity: Birth before 37 completed weeks' gestation; also known as preterm.

Recumbent position: reclining or lying down.

Respiratory Distress Syndrome (RDS): a disease of premature infants that results from immaturity of the respiratory system.

Small-for-gestational age (SGA): birthweight that is below the 10th percentile for gestational age; also known as intrauterine growth retardation (IUGR).

Spontaneous abortion: loss of a pregnancy before 24 weeks' gestation without any apparent cause.

Stillborn: an infant born dead.

Sudden Infant Death Syndrome (SIDS): the unexpected and unexplained death of an apparently well infant.

Supine position: lying on the back, face upward.

Underweight: weight-for-height before pregnancy of 90 percent or less.

Uterus: the organ that receives and holds the fertilized egg during pregnancy; also known as the womb.

Very low birthweight: birthweight less than 1,500 grams (3 pounds 4 ounces).

Zygote: the fertilized egg.

Notes

Chapter 2. Traditional Risk Factors:
What Your Doctor Is Likely to Ask You

1. McGrady GA, Sung JFC, Rowley DL, and Hogue CJR. Preterm delivery and low birthweight among first-born infants of black and white college graduates. *American Journal of Epidemiology.* 1992; 136:266–276.
2. Cabral H, Fried LE, Levenson S, Amaro H, and Zuckerman B. Foreign-born and U.S.-born black women: Differences in health behaviors and birth outcomes. *American Journal of Public Health.* 1990; 80:70–72.
3. Kleinman JC, Fingerhut LA, and Prager K. Differences in infant mortality by race, nativity status, and other maternal characteristics. *American Journal of Diseases of Children.* 1991; 145:194–199.

4. Teenage pregnancy and birth rates—United States, 1990. *Morbidity and Mortality Weekly Report.* 1993; 42:733–737.

5. Naeye RL. Teenaged and pre-teenaged pregnancies: Consequences of the fetal-maternal competition for nutrients. *Pediatrics.* 1981; 67:146–150.

6. Frisancho AR, Matos J, and Flegel P. Maternal nutritional status and adolescent pregnancy outcome. *American Journal of Clinical Nutrition.* 1983; 38:739–746.

7. Frisancho AR, Matos J, and Bollettino LA. Role of gynecological age and growth maturity status in fetal maturation and prenatal growth of infants born to young, still-growing adolescent mothers. *Human Biology.* 1984; 56:583–593.

8. Scholl TO, Hediger ML, and Ances IG. Maternal growth during pregnancy and decreased infant birthweight. *American Journal of Clinical Nutrition.* 1990; 51:790–793.

9. Maso MJ, Gong EJ, Jacobson MS, Bross DS, and Heald FP. Anthropometric predictors of low birthweight outcome in teenage pregnancy. *Journal of Adolescent Health Care.* 1988; 9:188–193.

10. Moerman ML. Growth of the birth canal in adolescent girls. *American Journal of Obstetrics and Gynecology.* 1982; 143:528–532.

11. Zlatnik FJ and Burmeister LF. Low "gynecologic" age: An obstetric risk factor. *American Journal of Obstetrics and Gynecology.* 1977; 128:183–186.

12. Scholl TO, Salmon RW, Miller LK, Vasilenko P, Furey CH, and Christine SrM. Weight gain during adolescent pregnancy. *Journal of Adolescent Health Care.* 1988; 9:286–290.

13. Horon IL, Strobino DM, and MacDonald HM. Birthweights among infants born to adolescent and young adult women. *American Journal of Obstetrics and Gynecology.* 1983; 146:444–449.

14. Unintended pregnancy—New York, 1988–1989. *Morbidity and Mortality Weekly Report.* 1991; 40:723–725.

15. Ventura SJ. Trends and variations in first births to older women, 1970–86. National Center for Health Statistics, *Vital and Health Statistics.* Vol. 21, No. 47, 1989.

16. Ventura SJ, Martin JA, Taffel SM, et al. Advance report of final natality statistics, 1992. *Monthly Vital Statistics Report.* Vol. 43, No. 5, Suppl., Hyattsville, Md.: National Center for Health Statistics, 1994.

17. Fonteyn VJ and Isada NB. Nongenetic implications of child-bearing after age thirty-five. *Obstetrical and Gynecological Review.* 1988; 43:709–720.

18. Taffel S. Maternal weight gain and the outcome of pregnancy, United States, 1980. *Vital and Health Statistics.* Vol. 21, No. 44, Hyattsville, Md.: National Center for Health Statistics, 1986.

19. Prager K, Malin H, Spiegler D, Van Natta P, and Placek P. Smoking and drinking behavior before and during pregnancy of married mothers of live-born infants and stillborn infants. *Public Health Reports.* 1984; 99:117–127.

20. Cnattingius S, Berendes HW, and Forman MR. Do delayed childbearers face increased risks of adverse pregnancy outcomes after the first birth? *Obstetrics and Gynecology.* 1993; 81:512–516.

21. Yasin SY and Beydoun SN. Pregnancy outcome at ≥20 weeks' gestation in women in their 40s: A case-control study. *Journal of Reproductive Medicine.* 1988; 33:209–213.

22. Forman MR, Meirik O, and Berendes HW. Delayed child-bearing in Sweden. *Journal of the American Medical Association.* 1984; 252:3135–3139.

23. Aldous MB and Edmonson MB. Maternal age at first childbirth and risk of low birthweight and preterm delivery in Washington State. *Journal of the American Medical Association.* 1993; 270:2574–2577.

24. Cnattingius S, Forman MR, Berendes HW, and Isotalo L. Delayed childbearing and risk of adverse perinatal outcome. *Journal of the American Medical Association.* 1992; 268:886–890.

25. Berkowitz GS, Skovron ML, Lapinski RH, and Berkowitz RL. Delayed childbearing and the outcome of pregnancy. *New England Journal of Medicine.* 1990; 322:659–664.

26. Barkan SE and Bracken MB. Delayed childbearing: No evidence for increased risk of low birthweight and preterm delivery. *American Journal of Epidemiology.* 1987; 125:101–109.

27. Lee K-S, Ferguson RM, Corpuz M, and Gartner LM. Maternal age and incidence of low birthweight at term: A population study. *American Journal of Obstetrics and Gynecology.* 1988; 158:84–89.

28. Pickering RM and Forbes JF. Risks of preterm delivery and small-for-gestational age infants following abortion: A popu-

lation study. *British Journal of Obstetrics and Gynaecology.* 1985; 92:1106–1112.

29. Thom DH, Nelson LM, and Vaughn TL. Spontaneous abortion and subsequent adverse birth outcomes. *American Journal of Obstetrics and Gynecology.* 1992; 166:111–116.

30. Reginald PW, Beard RW, Chapple J, Forbes PB, Liddell HS, Mowbray JF, and Underwood JL. Outcome of pregnancies progressing beyond 28 weeks' gestation in women with a history of recurrent miscarriage. *British Journal of Obstetrics and Gynaecology.* 1987; 94:643–648.

31. Strobino B, Fox HE, Kline J, Stein Z, Susser M, and Warburton D. Characteristics of women with recurrent spontaneous abortions and women with favorable reproductive histories. *American Journal of Public Health.* 1986; 76: 986–991.

32. Goldenberg RL, Mayberry SK, Copper RL, Dubard MB, and Hauth JC. Pregnancy outcome following a second-trimester loss. *Obstetrics and Gynecology.* 1993; 81:444–446.

33. Berkowitz GS. An epidemiologic study of preterm birth. *American Journal of Epidemiology.* 1981; 113:81–92.

34. Lumley J. Very low birth-weight (<1500 g) and previous induced abortion: Victoria 1982–1983. *Australian and New Zealand Journal of Obstetrics and Gynaecology.* 1986; 26:268–272.

35. Mandelson MT, Moden CB, and Daling JR. Low birthweight in relation to multiple induced abortions. *American Journal of Public Health.* 1992; 82:391–394.

36. Bakketeig LS, Hoffman HJ, and Harley EE. The tendency to repeat gestational age and birthweight in successive births. *American Journal of Obstetrics and Gynecology.* 1979; 135:1086–1103.

37. Wilcox LS and Mosher WD. Use of infertility services in the United States. *Obstetrics and Gynecology.* 1993; 82:122–127.

38. Cohen J, Mayaux MJ, and Guihard-Moscato ML. Pregnancy outcomes after in vitro fertilization: A collaborative study on 2,342 pregnancies. *Annals of the New York Academy of Sciences.* 1988; 541:1–6.

39. Herbst AL, Hubby MM, Azizi F, and Makii MM. Reproductive and gynecologic surgical experience in diethylstilbestrol-exposed daughters. *American Journal of Obstetrics and Gynecology.* 1981; 141:1019–1026.

40. Stillman RJ. In utero exposure to diethylstilbestrol: Adverse effects on the reproductive tract and reproductive performance in male and female offspring. *American Journal of Obstetrics and Gynecology.* 1982; 142:905–921.
41. Harger JH, Hsing AW, Tuomala RE, Gibbs RS, Mead PB, Eschenbach DA, Knox GE, and Polk BF. Risk factors for preterm premature rupture of fetal membranes: A multicenter case-control study. *American Journal of Obstetrics and Gynecology.* 1990; 163:130–137.
42. Gibbs RS, Romero R, Hiller SL, Eschenbach DA, and Sweet RL. A review of premature birth and subclinical infection. *American Journal of Obstetrics and Gynecology.* 1992; 166:1515–1528.
43. Luke B. The changing pattern of multiple births in the United States: Maternal and infant characteristics, 1973 and 1990. *Obstetrics and Gynecology.* 1994; 84:101–106.
44. Luke B and Keith LG. The contribution of singletons, twins, and triplets to low birthweight, infant mortality and handicap in the United States. *Journal of Reproductive Medicine.* 1992; 37:661–666.

Chapter 3. The Physiology of Preterm Labor: What's Going On in Your Body?

1. Kerr MG, Scott DB, and Samuel E. Studies of the inferior vena cava in late pregnancy. *British Medical Journal.* 1964; 1:532–533.
2. Schneider KTM, Bollinger A, Huch A, and Huch R. The oscillating "vena cava syndrome" during quiet standing—An unexpected observation in late pregnancy. *British Journal of Obstetrics and Gynaecology.* 1984; 91:766–780.
3. Schneider KTM, Huch A, and Huch R. Premature contractions: Are they caused by maternal standing? *Acta Genet. Med. Gemellol.* 1985; 34:175–178.
4. Schneider KTM, Bung P, Weber S, Huch A, and Huch R. An orthostatic uterovascular syndrome—A prospective, longitudinal study. *American Journal of Obstetrics and Gynecology.* 1993; 169:183–188.
5. Suonio S, Simpanen AL, and Olkkonen H. Effect of the left

lateral recumbent position compared with the supine and upright positions on placental blood flow in normal late pregnancy. *Annals of Clinical Research.* 1976; 8:22–28.

6. Naeye RL and Peters EC. Working during pregnancy: Effects on the fetus. *Pediatrics.* 1982; 69:724–727.

7. Council on Scientific Affairs. Effects of pregnancy on work performance. *Journal of the American Medical Association.* 1984; 251:1995–1997.

8. Schneider SM, Wright RG, Levinson G, Roizen MF, Wallis KL, Rolbin SH, and Craft JB. Uterine blood flow and plasma norepinephrine changes during maternal stress in the pregnant ewe. *Anesthesiology.* 1979; 50:524–527.

9. Adamsons K, Mueller-Heubach E, and Myers RE. Production of fetal asphyxia in the rhesus monkey by administration of catecholamines to the mother. *American Journal of Obstetrics and Gynecology.* 1971; 109:248–262.

10. Zuspan FP. Catecholamines: Their role in pregnancy and the development of pregnancy-induced hypertension. *Journal of Reproductive Medicine.* 1979; 23:143–150.

11. Homer CJ, James SA, and Siegel E. Work-related psychosocial stress and risk of preterm, low birthweight delivery. *American Journal of Public Health.* 1990; 80:173–177.

12. Omer H and Everly GS. Psychological factors in preterm labor: Critical review and theoretical synthesis. *American Journal of Psychiatry.* 1988; 145:1507–1513.

13. Newton RW and Hunt LP. Psychosocial stress in pregnancy and its relation to low birthweight. *British Medical Journal.* 1984; 288:1191–1194.

14. Omer H, Elizur Y, Barnea T, Friedlander D, and Polti Z. Psychological variables and premature labour: A possible solution for some methodological problems. *Journal of Psychosomatic Research.* 1986; 30:559–565.

Chapter 4. Your Home and Work Environments

1. Women in the labor force. *Statistical Bulletin of the Metropolitan Life Insurance Company.* 1994; 75:2–10.

2. U.S. Department of Labor, Bureau of Labor Statistics. *Working women: A chartbook.* Bulletin 2385. Washington, D.C., 1991.

3. Murphy JF, Newcombe R, Douncey M, Garcia J, and Elbourne D. Employment in pregnancy: Prevalence, maternal characteristics, perinatal outcome. *Lancet.* 1984; 1:1163–1166.

4. Marbury MC, Linn S, Monson RR, Wegman DH, Schoenbaum SC, Stubblefield PG, and Ryan KJ. Work and pregnancy. *Journal of Occupational Medicine.* 1984; 26:415–421.

5. Gofin J. The effect on birthweight of employment during pregnancy. *Journal of Biosocial Science.* 1979; 11:259–267.

6. Savitz DA, Whelan EA, Rowland AS, and Kleckner RC. Maternal employment and reproductive risk factors. *American Journal of Epidemiology.* 1990; 132:933–945.

7. Klebanoff MA, Shiono PH, and Rhoades GG. Outcomes of pregnancy in a national sample of resident physicians. *New England Journal of Medicine.* 1990; 323:1040–1045.

8. Miller NH, Katz VL, and Cefalo RC. Pregnancies among physicians: A historical cohort study. *Journal of Reproductive Medicine.* 1989; 34:790–796.

9. Grunebaum A, Minkoff H, and Blake D. Pregnancy among obstetricians: A comparison of births before, during, and after residency. *American Journal of Obstetrics and Gynecology.* 1987; 157:79–83.

10. Luke B, Keith LG, Minogue J, Mamelle N, Papiernik E, and Johnson TRB. Work during pregnancy: The association between occupational fatigue, obstetrical history, and preterm birth. Fortieth Annual Clinical Meeting, the American College of Obstetricians and Gynecologists, Las Vegas, Nevada, April 1992.

11. Saurel-Cubizolles MJ, Kaminski M, Ilado-Arkhipoff J, Du Mazaubrun C, Estryn-Behar M, Berthier C, Mouchet M, and Kelfa C. Pregnancy and its outcome among hospital personnel according to occupation and working conditions. *Journal of Epidemiology and Community Health.* 1985; 39:129–134.

12. Ramirez G, Grimes RM, Annegers JF, Davis BR, and Slater CH. Occupational physical activity and other risk factors for preterm birth among US Army primigravidas. *American Journal of Public Health.* 1990; 80:728–729.

13. Fox ME, Harris RE, and Brekken AL. The active-duty military pregnancy: A new high-risk category. *American Journal of Obstetrics and Gynecology.* 1977; 129:705–707.

14. Adams MA, Harlass FE, Sarno AP, Read JA, and Rawlings JS. Antenatal hospitalization among enlisted servicewomen, 1987–1990. *Obstetrics and Gynecology.* 1994; 84:35–39.
15. Launer LJ, Villar J, Kestler E, and DeOnis M. The effect of maternal work on fetal growth and duration of pregnancy: A prospective study. *British Journal of Obstetrics and Gynaecology.* 1990; 97:62–70.
16. Teitelman AM, Welch LS, Hellenbrand KG, and Bracken MB. Effect of maternal work activity on preterm birth and low birthweight. *American Journal of Epidemiology.* 1990; 131:104–113.
17. Saurel-Cubizolles MJ, Kaminski M, Du Mazaubrun C, Llado J, and Estryn-Behar M. High blood pressure during pregnancy and working conditions among hospital personnel. *European Journal of Obstetrics and Gynecology and Reproductive Biology.* 1991; 40:29–34.
18. Naeye RL and Peters EC. Working during pregnancy: Effects on the fetus. *Pediatrics.* 1982; 69:724–727.
19. Klebanoff MA, Shiono PH, and Carey JC. The effect of physical activity during pregnancy on preterm delivery and birthweight. *American Journal of Obstetrics and Gynecology.* 1990; 163:1450–1456.
20. Saurel-Cubizolles MJ, Subtil D, and Kaminski M. Is preterm delivery still related to physical working conditions in pregnancy? *Journal of Epidemiology and Community Health.* 1991; 45:29–34.
21. Mamelle N, Laumon B, and Lazar P. Prematurity and occupational activity during pregnancy. *American Journal of Epidemiology.* 1984; 119:309–322.
22. Kerr MG, Scott DB, and Samuel E. Studies of the inferior vena cava in late pregnancy. *British Medical Journal.* 1964; 1:532–533.
23. Schneider KTM, Bollinger A, Huch A, and Huch R. The oscillating "vena cava syndrome" during quiet standing—An unexpected observation in late pregnancy. *British Journal of Obstetrics and Gynaecology.* 1984; 91:766–780.
24. Schneider KTM, Huch A, and Huch R. Premature contractions: Are they caused by maternal standing? *Acta Genet. Med. Gemellol.* 1985; 34:175–178.
25. Schneider KTM, Bung P, Weber S, Huch A, and Huch R. An orthostatic uterovascular syndrome—A prospective, lon-

gitudinal study. *American Journal of Obstetrics and Gynecology.* 1993; 169:183–188.

26. Suonio S, Simpanen AL, and Olkkonen H. Effect of the left lateral recumbent position compared with the supine and upright positions on placental blood flow in normal late pregnancy. *Annals of Clinical Research.* 1976; 8:22–28.

27. Armstrong BG, Nolin AD, and McDonald AD. Work in pregnancy and birthweight for gestational age. *British Journal of Industrial Medicine.* 1989; 46:196–199.

28. McDonald AD, McDonald JC, Armstrong B, Cherry NM, Nolin AD, and Robert D. Prematurity and work in pregnancy. *British Journal of Industrial Medicine.* 1988; 45:56–62.

29. Peoples-Sheps MD, Siegel E, Suchindran CM, Origasa H, Ware A, and Barakat A. Characteristics of maternal employment during pregnancy: Effects on low birthweight. *American Journal of Public Health.* 1991; 81:1007–1012.

30. Office of Technology Assessment. *Biological Rhythms: Implications for the Worker.* OTA–BA–463. Washington, D.C.: U.S. Congress, Office of Technology Assessment, Sep. 1991.

31. Axelsson G, Rylander R, and Molin I. Outcome of pregnancy in relation to irregular and inconvenient work schedules. *British Journal of Industrial Medicine.* 1989; 46:393–398.

32. Nurminen T. Shift work, fetal development, and course of pregnancy. *Scandinavian Journal of Work and Environmental Health.* 1989; 15:395–403.

33. Timio M, Gentili S, and Pede S. Free adrenaline and noradrenaline excretion related to occupational stress. *British Heart Journal.* 1979; 42:471–474.

34. Fibiger W, Singer G, and Miller AJ. Relationships between catecholamines in urine and physical and mental effort. *International Journal of Psychophysiology.* 1984; 1:325–333.

35. Sundin T. The effect of body posture on the urinary excretion of adrenaline and noradrenaline. *Acta Medica Scandinavica.* 1958; 161: Suppl. 336.

36. von Euler US and Hellner S. Noradrenaline excretion in muscular work. *Acta Physiologia Scandinavica.* 1952; 26:183–191.

37. Dimsdale JE and Moss J. Plasma catecholamines in stress and exercise. *Journal of the American Medical Association.* 1980; 243:340–342.

38. Katz VL, Jenkins T, Haley L, and Bowes WA. Cate-

Notes

cholamine levels in pregnant physicians and nurses: A pilot
study of stress and pregnancy. *Obstetrics and Gynecology.*
1991; 77:338–342.

39. Shnider SM, Wright RG, Levinson G, Roizen MF, Wallis
KL, Rolbin SH, and Craft JB. Uterine blood flow and
plasma norepinephrine changes during maternal stress in the
pregnant ewe. *Anesthesiology.* 1979; 50:524–527.

Chapter 5. Your Lifestyle: Risks and Rewards

1. Schoenborn CA, and Cohen BH. *Trends in smoking, alcohol
consumption, and other health practices among U.S. adults, 1977
and 1983.* DHHS Publication No. (PHS) 86–1250. Hyattsville, Md.: National Center for Health Statistics, 1986.
2. Centers for Disease Control. Frequent alcohol consumption
among women of childbearing age—Behavioral risk factor
surveillance system, 1991. *Morbidity and Mortality Weekly
Report.* 1994; 43:328–335.
3. Hook EB. Dietary cravings and aversions during pregnancy.
American Journal of Clinical Nutrition. 1978; 31:1355–1362.
4. Kim I, Hungerford DW, Yip R, Kuester SA, Zyrkowski C,
and Trowbridge FL. Pregnancy nutrition surveillance system—United States, 1979–1990. *Morbidity and Mortality
Weekly Report.* 1992; 41:SS–7, 25–41.
5. Frezza M, di Padova C, Pozzato G, et al. High blood alcohol
levels in women: The role of decreased gastric alcohol dehydrogenase activity and first-pass metabolism. *New England
Journal of Medicine.* 1990; 322:95–99.
6. Ashley MJ, Olin JS, le Riche WH, et al. Morbidity in al-
coholics: Evidence for accelerated development of physical
disease in women. *Archives of Internal Medicine.* 1977;
137:883–887.
7. Saunders JB, Davis M, and Williams R. Do women develop
alcoholic liver disease more readily than men? *British Medical
Journal.* 1981; 282:1140–1143.
8. Norton R, Batey R, Dwyer T, and MacMahon S. Alcohol
consumption and the risk of alcohol-related cirrhosis in
women. *British Medical Journal.* 1987; 295:80–82.
9. Mello NK. Some behavioral and biological aspects of alco-

208

hol problems in women. In Kalant OJ (ed), *Alcohol and Drug Problems in Women.* New York: Plenum Press, 1980; 263–298.

10. Cicero TJ. Sex differences in the effects of alcohol and other psychoactive drugs on endocrine function: Clinical and experimental evidence. In Kalant OJ (ed), *Alcohol and Drug Problems in Women.* New York: Plenum Press 1980; 545–593.

11. Armstrong BG, McDonald AD, and Sloan A. Cigarette, alcohol, and coffee consumption and spontaneous abortion. *American Journal of Public Health.* 1992; 82:85–87.

12. Lemoine P, Harrousseau H, Borteyru JP, and Menuet J. Les enfants de parents alcooliques: Anomalies observées. A propos de 127 cas. *Quest. Med.* 1968; 25:476–482.

13. Jones KL, Smith DW, Ulleland CN, et al. Pattern of malformation in offspring of chronic alcoholic mothers. *Lancet.* 1973; 1:1267–1271.

14. Streissguth AP, Sampson PD, Barr HM, et al. Studying alcohol teratogenesis from the perspective of the fetal alcohol syndrome: Methodological and statistical issues. *Annals of the New York Academy of Sciences.* 1986; 477:63–86.

15. Abel EL and Sokol RJ. Incidence of fetal alcohol syndrome and economic impact of FAS-related anomalies. *Drug and Alcohol Dependency.* 1987; 19:51–70.

16. Streissguth AP, Landesman-Dwyer S, Martin JC, and Smith DW. Teratogenic effects of alcohol in humans and laboratory animals. *Science.* 1980; 209:353–361.

17. Luke B. The fetal alcohol syndrome. *American Journal of Nursing.* 1977; 77:1924–1927.

18. Larroque B, Kaminski M, Lelong N, Subtil D, and Dehaene P. Effects on birthweight of alcohol and caffeine consumption during pregnancy. *American Journal of Epidemiology.* 1993; 137:941–950.

19. Ernhart CB, Sokol RJ, Martier S, et al. Alcohol teratogenicity in the human: A detailed assessment of specificity, critical period, and threshold. *American Journal of Obstetrics and Gynecology.* 1987; 156:33–39.

20. Kaminski M, Rumeau C, and Schwartz D. Alcohol consumption in pregnant women and the outcome of pregnancy. *Alcoholism: Clinical and Experimental Research.* 1978; 2: 155–163.

21. Streissguth AP, Barr HM, Sampson PD, et al. IQ at age 4 in relation to maternal alcohol use and smoking during pregnancy. *Developmental Psychology.* 1989; 25:3–11.

22. Kennedy LA. The pathogenesis of brain abnormalities in the fetal alcohol syndrome: An integrating hypothesis. *Teratology.* 1984; 29:363–368.

23. Pikkarainen PH and Raiha NC. Development of alcohol dehydrogenase activity in the human liver. *Pediatric Research.* 1967; 1:165–168

24. Brien JF, Loomis CW, Tranmer J, and McGrath H. Disposition of ethanol in human maternal venous blood and amniotic fluid. *American Journal of Obstetrics and Gynecology.* 1983; 146:181–186.

25. Fisher SE. Ethanol: Effect on fetal brain growth and development. In Tarter RE and Van Thiel DH (eds), *Alcohol and the Brain: Chronic Effects.* New York: Plenum Press, 1985; 265–281.

26. Streissguth AP, Aase JM, Clarren SK, et al. Fetal alcohol syndrome in adolescents and adults. *Journal of the American Medical Association.* 1991; 265:1961–1967.

27. U.S. Department of Health and Human Services. *The health benefits of smoking cessation: A report of the Surgeon General.* U.S. Department of Health and Human Services publication No. (CDC) 90–8416, 1990.

28. U.S. Department of Health and Human Services. *Reducing the health consequences of smoking: 25 years of progress: A report of the Surgeon General.* U.S. Department of Health and Human Services publication No. (CDC) 89–8411, 1989.

29. Centers for Disease Control. Cigarette smoking among adults—United States, 1990. *Morbidity and Mortality Weekly Report.* 1992; 41:354–362.

30. Shapiro S, Slone D, Rosenberg L, et al. Oral contraceptive use in relation to myocardial infarction. *Lancet.* 1979; 1: 743–747.

31. Centers for Disease Control. Cigarette smoking among reproductive-aged women—Behavioral risk factor surveillance system, 1989. *Morbidity and Mortality Weekly Report.* 1991; 40:719–723.

32. Olsen J. Cigarette smoking, tea and coffee drinking, and subfecundity. *American Journal of Epidemiology.* 1991; 133:734–739.

33. Martin TR and Bracken MB. The association between low birthweight and caffeine consumption during pregnancy. *American Journal of Epidemiology.* 1987; 126:813–821.

34. Mills JL, Holmes LB, Aarons JH, Simpson JL, Brown ZA, et al. Moderate caffeine use and the risk of spontaneous abortion and intrauterine growth retardation. *Journal of the American Medical Association.* 1993; 269:593–597.

35. Mattison DR, Plowchalk DR, Meadows MJ, Miller MM, Malek A, and London S. The effect of smoking on oogenesis, fertilization, and implantation. *Seminars in Reproductive Endocrinology.* 1989; 7:291–304.

36. Chow W-H, Daling JR, Weiss NS, and Voigt LF. Maternal cigarette smoking and tubal pregnancy. *Obstetrics and Gynecology.* 1988; 71:167–170.

37. Campbell OM and Gray RH. Smoking and ectopic pregnancy: A multinational case-control study. In Rosenberg MJ (ed), *Smoking and Reproductive Health*. Littleton, Mass.: PSG Publishing, 1987:70–75.

38. Kline J, Stein ZA, Susser M, and Warburton D. Smoking: A risk factor for spontaneous abortion. *New England Journal of Medicine.* 1977; 297:793–796.

39. Harlap S and Shiono PH. Alcohol, smoking, and incidence of spontaneous abortions in the first and second trimester. *Lancet.* 1980; 2:173–176.

40. Pattison HA, Taylor PJ, and Pattison MH. The effect of cigarette smoking on ovarian function and early pregnancy outcome of in vitro fertilization treatment. *Fertility and Sterility.* 1991; 55:780–783.

41. Kline J, Levin B, Shrout P, Stein Z, Susser M, and Warburton D. Maternal smoking and trisomy among spontaneously aborted conceptions. *American Journal of Human Genetics.* 1983; 35:421–431.

42. Kulikauskas V, Blaustein D, and Ablin RJ. Cigarette smoking and its possible effects on sperm. *Fertility and Sterility.* 1985; 44:526–528.

43. Rosenberg MJ. Does smoking affect sperm? In Rosenberg MJ (ed), *Smoking and Reproductive Health*. Littleton, Mass.: PSG Publishing, 1987; 54–62.

44. Manning FA, and Feyerabend C. Cigarette smoking and fetal breathing movements. *British Journal of Obstetrics and Gynaecology.* 1976; 83:262–270.

45. Naeye RL. Abruptio placentae and placenta previa: Frequency, perinatal mortality, and cigarette smoking. *Obstetrics and Gynecology.* 1980; 55:701–704.

46. Cardozo LD, Gibb DMF, Studd JWW, and Cooper DJ. Social and obstetric features associated with smoking in pregnancy. *British Journal of Obstetrics and Gynaecology.* 1982; 89:622–627.

47. Meyer MB, Jonas BS, and Tonascia JA. Perinatal events associated with maternal smoking during pregnancy. *American Journal of Epidemiology.* 1976; 103:464–476.

48. Naeye RL. Factors that predispose to premature rupture of the fetal membranes. *Obstetrics and Gynecology.* 1982; 60:93–98.

49. Hadley CB, Main DM, and Gabbe SG. Risk factors for preterm premature rupture of the fetal membranes. *American Journal of Perinatology.* 1990; 7:374–379.

50. Harger JH, Hsing AW, Tuomala RE, Gibbs RS, Mead PB, Eschenbach DA, et al. Risk factors for preterm premature rupture of fetal membranes: A multicenter case-control study. *American Journal of Obstetrics and Gynecology.* 1990; 163:130–137.

51. Williams MA, Mittendorf R, Stubblefield PG, Lieberman E, Schoenbaum SC, and Monson RR. Cigarettes, coffee, and preterm premature rupture of the membranes. *American Journal of Epidemiology.* 1992; 135:895–903.

52. Simpson WJ. A preliminary report of cigarette smoking and the incidence of prematurity. *American Journal of Obstetrics and Gynecology.* 1957; 73:808–815.

53. McDonald AD, Armstrong BG, and Sloan M. Cigarette, alcohol, and coffee consumption and prematurity. *American Journal of Public Health.* 1992; 82:87–90.

54. Shiono PH, Klebanoff MA, and Rhoades GG. Smoking and drinking during pregnancy: Their effects on preterm birth. *Journal of the American Medical Association.* 1986; 255:82–84.

55. Lieberman E, Ryan KJ, Monson RR, and Schoenbaum SC. Risk factors accounting for racial differences in the rate of premature birth. *New England Journal of Medicine.* 1987; 317:743–748.

56. Wen SW, Goldenberg RL, Cutter GR, Hoffman HJ, and Cliver SP. Intrauterine growth retardation and preterm deliv-

ery: Prenatal risk factors in an indigent population. *American Journal of Obstetrics and Gynecology.* 1990; 162:213–218.

57. Hartikainen-Sorri A-L and Sorri M. Occupational and socio-medical factors in preterm birth. *Obstetrics and Gynecology.* 1989; 74:13–16.

58. Haworth JC, Ellestad-Sayed JJ, King J, and Dilling LA. Fetal growth retardation in cigarette-smoking mothers is not due to decreased maternal food intake. *American Journal of Obstetrics and Gynecology.* 1980; 137:719–723.

59. Ounsted M, Moar VA, and Scott A. Risk factors associated with small-for-dates and large-for-dates infants. *British Journal of Obstetrics and Gynaecology.* 1985; 92:226–232.

60. MacArthur C and Knox EG. Smoking in pregnancy: Effects of stopping at different stages. *British Journal of Obstetrics and Gynaecology.* 1988; 95:551–555.

61. Lieberman E, Gremy I, Lang JM, and Cohen AP. Low birth-weight at term and the timing of fetal exposure to maternal smoking. *American Journal of Public Health.* 1994; 84:1127–1131.

62. Fox SH, Koepsell TD, and Daling JR. Birthweight and smoking during pregnancy—Effect modification by maternal age. *American Journal of Epidemiology.* 1994; 139:1008–1015.

63. Kuhnert BR, Kuhnert PM, Debanne S, and Williams TG. The relationship between cadmium, zinc, and birthweight in pregnant women who smoke. *American Journal of Obstetrics and Gynecology.* 1987; 157:1247–1251.

64. Webster WS. Cadmium-induced fetal growth retardation in the mouse. *Archives of Environmental Health.* 1978; 33:36–42.

65. Rintahaka PJ and Hirvonen J. The epidemiology of sudden infant death syndrome in Finland in 1969–1980. *Forensic Science International.* 1986; 30:219–233.

66. Schectman G, Byrd JC, and Hoffmann R. Ascorbic acid requirements for smokers: Analysis of a population survey. *American Journal of Clinical Nutrition.* 1991; 53:1466–1470.

67. Bendich, A. Importance of vitamin status to pregnancy outcomes. In Bendich A and Butterworth CE (eds), *Micronutrients in Health and Disease.* New York: Marcel Dekker, 1991; 235–262.

68. Norkus EP, Hsu H, and Cehelsky MR. Effect of cigarette smoking on the vitamin C status of pregnant women and

their offspring. *Annals of the New York Academy of Sciences.* 1987; 498:500–501.

69. Norkus EP, Hsu HW, Leighton LS, and Cehelsky MR. Relationship between cigarette smoking and plasma levels of vitamin E and beta carotene in pregnant women and newborn infants. *FASEB Journal.* 1989; 3:A766.

70. American College of Obstetricians and Gynecologists. *Smoking and Reproductive Health.* Technical Bulletin No. 180, May 1993.

71. Knutti R, Rothweiler H, and Schlatter C. The effect of pregnancy on the pharmacokinetics of caffeine. *Archives of Toxicology* (Supplement) 1982; 5:187–192.

72. Nishimura H and Nakai K. Congenital malformations in offspring of mice treated with caffeine. *Proceedings of the Society for Experimental Biology and Medicine.* 1960; 104:140–142.

73. Nolen GA. The developmental toxicology of caffeine. *Issues and Review of Teratology.* 1988; 4:305–350.

74. Soyka LF. Effects of methylxanthines on the fetus. *Clinics in Perinatology.* 1979; 6:37–51.

75. Gilbert EF, Pistey WR. Effect on the offspring of repeated caffeine administration to pregnant rats. *Journal of Reproduction and Fertility.* 1973; 34:495–499.

76. Food and Drug Administration. *Report on caffeine.* Washington, D.C.: U.S. Government Printing Office, 1980.

77. Food and Nutrition Board, Committee on the Mother and Preschool Child. *Alternative Dietary Practices and Nutritional Abuses in Pregnancy.* Washington, D.C.: National Academy of Sciences, 1982.

78. Wilcox A, Weinberg C, and Baird D. Caffeinated beverages and decreased fertility. *Lancet.* 1988; 2:1453–1456.

79. Christianson RE, Oechsli FW, and Van den Berg BJ. Caffeinated beverages and decreased fertility. *Lancet.* 1989; 1:378.

80. Williams MA, Monson RR, Goldman MB, Mettendorf R, and Ryan KJ. Coffee and delayed conception. *Lancet.* 1990; 1:1603.

81. Hatch EE and Bracken MB. Association of delayed conception with caffeine consumption. *American Journal of Epidemiology.* 1993; 138:1082–1092.

82. Grodstein F, Goldman MB, Ryan L, and Cramer DW. Relation of female infertility to consumption of caffeinated beverages. *American Journal of Epidemiology*. 1993; 137:1353–1360.

83. Furuhashi N, Sato S, Suzuki M, Hiruta M, Tanaka M, and Takahashi T. Effects of caffeine ingestion during pregnancy. *Gynecological and Obstetrical Investigation*. 1985; 19:187–191.

84. Srisuphan W and Bracken MB. Caffeine consumption during pregnancy and association with late spontaneous abortion. *American Journal of Obstetrics and Gynecology*. 1986; 154:14–20.

85. Weathersbee PS, Olsen LK, and Lodge JR. Caffeine and pregnancy: A retrospective study. *Postgraduate Medicine*. 1977; 62:64–69.

86. Kurppa K, Holmberg PC, Kuosma E, and Saxen L. Coffee consumption during pregnancy and selected congenital malformations: A nationwide case-control study. *American Journal of Public Health*. 1983; 73:1397–1399.

87. Linn S, Schoenbaum SC, Monson RR, et al. No association between coffee consumption and adverse outcomes of pregnancy. *New England Journal of Medicine*. 1982; 306:141–145.

88. Rosenberg L, Mitchell AA, Shapiro S, and Slone D. Selected birth defects in relation to caffeine-containing beverages. *Journal of the American Medical Association*. 1982; 247: 1429–1432.

89. Tikkanen J and Heinonen OP. Cardiovascular malformations and organic solvent exposure during pregnancy in Finland. *American Journal of Industrial Medicine*. 1988; 14:1–8.

90. Borlee I, Lechat MF, Bouckaert A, and Misson C. Le café, facteur de risque pendant la grosse? *Louvain Medicine*. 1978; 97:279–284.

91. De Wals P and Lechat MF. EUROCAT Report 1: *Surveillance of congenital anomalies, years 1980–1983*. Brussels: Department of Epidemiology, Catholic University of Louvain, 1986.

92. McDonald AD, Armstrong BG, and Sloan M. Cigarette, alcohol, and coffee consumption and congenital defects. *American Journal of Public Health*. 1992; 82:91–93.

93. Muñoz L, Lonnderal B, Keen CL, and Dewey KG. Coffee consumption as a factor in iron-deficiency anemia among

pregnant women and their children in Costa Rica. *American Journal of Clinical Nutrition.* 1988; 48:645–651.

94. Caan BJ and Goldhaber MK. Caffeinated beverages and low birthweight: A case-control study. *American Journal of Public Health.* 1989; 79:1299–1300.

95. Brooke OG, Anderson HR, Bland JM, Peacock JL, and Stewart CM. Effects on birthweight of smoking, alcohol, caffeine, socioeconomic factors and psychosocial stress. *British Medical Journal.* 1989; 298:795–801.

96. Watkinson B and Fried PA. Maternal caffeine use before, during and after pregnancy and effects upon offspring. *Neurobehavioral Toxicology and Teratology.* 1985; 7:9–17.

97. Fortier I, Marcoux S, and Beaulac-Baillargeon L. Relation of caffeine intake during pregnancy to intrauterine growth retardation and preterm birth. *American Journal of Epidemiology.* 1993; 137:931–940.

98. Acheson KJ, Zahorska-Markiewicz B, Pittet P, Anantharaman K, and Jequier E. Caffeine and coffee: Their influence on metabolic rate and substrate utilization in normal weight and obese individuals. *American Journal of Clinical Nutrition.* 1980; 33:989–997.

99. Hollands MA, Arch JRS, and Cawthrone MA. A simple apparatus for comparative measurements of energy expenditure in human subjects: The thermic effect of caffeine. *American Journal of Clinical Nutrition.* 1981; 34:2291–2294.

100. Jung RT, Shetty PS, James WPT, Barrand MA, and Callingham BA. Caffeine: Its effect on catecholamines and metabolism in lean and obese subjects. *Clinical Science.* 1981; 60:527–535.

101. Astrup A, Toubro S, Cannon S, Hein P, Breum L, and Madsen J. Caffeine: A double-blind, placebo-controlled study of its thermogenic, metabolic, and cardiovascular effects in healthy volunteers. *American Journal of Clinical Nutrition.* 1990; 51:759–767.

102. Kirkinen P, Jouppila P, Koivula A, Vuori J, and Puukka M. The effect of caffeine on placental and fetal blood flow in human pregnancy. *American Journal of Obstetrics and Gynecology.* 1983; 147:939–942.

103. Miller RC, Watson WJ, Hackney AC, and Seeds JW. Acute maternal and fetal cardiovascular effects of caffeine ingestion. *American Journal of Perinatology.* 1994; 11:132–136.

104. Robertson D, Wade D, Workman RL, et al. Tolerance to the humoral and hemodynamic effects of caffeine in man. *Journal of Clinical Investigation.* 1981; 67:1111–1117.

105. Smits P, Thien T, and van't Laar A. Circulatory effects of coffee in relation to the pharmokinetics of caffeine. *American Journal of Cardiology.* 1985; 56:958–963.

106. Berkowitz GS, Holford TR, and Berkowitz RL. Effects of cigarette smoking, alcohol, coffee and tea consumption of preterm delivery. *Early Human Development.* 1982; 7: 239–245.

107. Narod SA, de Sanjose S, and Victoria C. Coffee during pregnancy: A reproductive hazard? *American Journal of Obstetrics and Gynecology.* 1991; 164:1109–1114.

108. Artal R, Platt LD, Sperling M, Kammula RK, Jilek J, and Nakamura R. Exercise in pregnancy. I. Maternal cardiovascular and metabolic responses in normal pregnancy. *American Journal of Obstetrics and Gynecology.* 1981; 140:123–127.

109. Dimsdale JE and Moss J. Plasma catecholamines in stress and exercise. *Journal of the American Medical Association.* 1980; 243:340–342.

110. Katz VL, Jenkins T, Haley L, and Bowes WA. Catecholamine levels in pregnant physicians and nurses: A pilot study of stress and pregnancy. *Obstetrics and Gynecology.* 1991; 77:338–342.

111. Fibiger W, Singer G, and Miller AJ. Relationships between catecholamines in urine and physical and mental effort. *International Journal of Psychophysiology.* 1984; 1:325–333.

112. American College of Obstetricians and Gynecologists. *Women and exercise.* ACOG Technical Bulletin No. 173. Washington, D.C.: ACOG, 1992.

113. American College of Obstetricians and Gynecologists. *Exercise during pregnancy and the postpartum period.* ACOG Technical Bulletin No. 189. Washington, D.C.: ACOG, 1994.

114. Clark SL, Cotton DB, Pivarnik JM, Lee W, Hankins GDV, Benedetti TJ, et al. Position change and central hemodynamic profile during normal third-trimester pregnancy and postpartum. *American Journal of Obstetrics and Gynecology.* 1991; 164:883–887.

115. Schneider KTM, Bollinger A, Huch A, and Huch R. The oscillating "vena cava syndrome" during quiet standing—an

unexpected observation in late pregnancy. *British Journal of Obstetrics and Gynaecology.* 1984; 91:766–780.

116. Schneider KTM, Bung P, Weber S, Huch A, and Huch R. An orthostatic uterovascular syndrome—A prospective longitudinal study. *American Journal of Obstetrics and Gynecology.* 1993; 169:183–188.

117. Edwards MJ. Hyperthermia as a teratogen: A review of experimental studies and their clinical significance. *Teratogenesis Carcinogenesis and Mutagenesis.* 1986; 6:563–582.

118. Milunsky A, Ulcickas M, Rothman KJ, Willett W, Jick SS, and Jick H. Maternal heat exposure and neural tube defects. *Journal of the American Medical Association.* 1992; 268: 882–885.

119. Clapp JF and Capeless EL. Neonatal morphometrics after endurance exercise during pregnancy. *American Journal of Obstetrics and Gynecology.* 1990; 163:1805–1811.

120. Clapp JF and Dickstein S. Endurance exercise and pregnancy outcome. *Medicine and Science in Sports and Exercise.* 1984; 16:556–562.

121. Morrow RJ, Ritchie JWK, and Bull SB. Fetal and maternal hemodynamic responses to exercise in pregnancy assessed by Doppler ultrasonography. *American Journal of Obstetrics and Gynecology.* 1989; 160:138–140.

122. Clapp JF. Acute exercise stress in the pregnant ewe. *American Journal of Obstetrics and Gynecology.* 1980; 136:489–494.

123. Clapp JF, Seaward BL, Sleamaker RH, and Hiser J. Maternal physiologic adaptations to early human pregnancy. *American Journal of Obstetrics and Gynecology.* 1988; 159:1456–1460.

124. Clapp JF. Exercise in pregnancy: A brief clinical review. *Fetal Medicine Review.* 1990; 2:89–101.

125. Collings CA, Curet LB, and Mullin JP. Maternal and fetal responses to a maternal aerobic exercise program. *American Journal of Obstetrics and Gynecology.* 1983; 145:702–707.

126. Clapp JF. The effects of maternal exercise on early pregnancy outcome. *American Journal of Obstetrics and Gynecology.* 1989; 161:1453–1457.

127. Artal R, Masaki DI, Khodiguian N, Romen Y, Rutherford SE, and Wiswell RA. Exercise prescription in pregnancy: Weight-bearing versus non-weight-bearing exercise. *American Journal of Obstetrics and Gynecology.* 1989; 161:1464–1469.

Notes

128. Sibley L, Ruhling RO, Cameron-Foster J, Christensen C, and Bolen T. Swimming and physical fitness during pregnancy. *Journal of Nurse-Midwifery.* 1981; 26:3–12.

Chapter 6. You (and Your Baby) Are What You Eat

1. Institute of Medicine. *Nutrition During Pregnancy.* Washington D.C.: National Academy Press, 1990.
2. Frisch RE (ed). *Adipose Tissue and Reproduction.* Basel, Switzerland: Karger, 1990.
3. Peckham CH and Christianson RE. The relationship between prepregnancy weight and certain obstetric factors. *American Journal of Obstetrics and Gynecology.* 1971; 111:1–7.
4. Brown JE, Jacobson HN, Askue LH, and Peick MG. Influence of pregnancy weight gain on the size of infants born to underweight women. *Obstetrics and Gynecology.* 1981; 57:13–17.
5. Mitchell MC and Lerner E. Weight gain and pregnancy outcome in underweight and normal weight women. *Journal of the American Dietetic Association.* 1989; 89:634–641.
6. Frentzen BH, Dimperio DL, and Cruz AC. Maternal weight gain: Effect on infant birthweight among overweight and average-weight low-income women. *American Journal of Obstetrics and Gynecology.* 1988; 159:1114–1117.
7. Wen SW, Goldenberg RL, Cutter GR, et al. Intrauterine growth retardation and preterm delivery: Prenatal risk factors in an indigent population. *American Journal of Obstetrics and Gynecology.* 1990; 162:213–218.
8. Abrams B and Newman V. Small-for-gestational age birth: Maternal predictors and comparison with risk factors of spontaneous preterm delivery in the same cohort. *American Journal of Obstetrics and Gynecology.* 1991; 164:785–790.
9. Berkowitz GS. An epidemiologic study of preterm delivery. *American Journal of Epidemiology.* 1981; 113:81–92.
10. Hediger ML, Scholl TO, Belsky DH, et al. Patterns of weight gain in adolescent pregnancy: Effects on birthweight and preterm delivery. *Obstetrics and Gynecology.* 1989; 74:6–12.
11. Abrams B, Newman V, Key T, and Parker J. Maternal weight

gain and preterm delivery. *Obstetrics and Gynecology.* 1989; 74:577–583.

12. Scholl TO, Hediger ML, Ances IG, Belsky DH, and Salmon RW. Weight gain during pregnancy in adolescence: Predictive ability of early weight gain. *Obstetrics and Gynecology.* 1990; 75:948–953.

13. Luke B, Minogue J, Abbey H, et al. The association between maternal weight gain and the birthweight of twins. *Journal of Maternal-Fetal Medicine.* 1992; 1:267-276.

14. Luke B, Minogue J, Keith L, Witter F, and Johnson TRB. The ideal twin pregnancy: Patterns of weight gain, discordancy, and length of gestation. *American Journal of Obstetrics and Gynecology.* 1993; 169:588–597.

15. Kaplan M, Eidelman AI, and Aboulafia Y. Fasting and the precipitation of labor: The Yom Kippur effect. *Journal of the American Medical Association.* 1983; 250:1317–1318.

16. Binienda Z, Massmann A, Mitchell MD, Gleed RD, Figueroa JP, and Nathanielsz PW. Effect of food withdrawal on arterial blood glucose and plasma 13, 14-dihydro-15-keto-prostaglandin $F_{2\alpha}$ concentrations and nocturnal myometrial electrographic activity in the pregnant rhesus monkey in the last trimester of gestation: A model for preterm labor? *American Journal of Obstetrics and Gynecology.* 1989; 160:746–750.

17. Garn SM, Ridella SA, Petzold AS, and Falkner F. Maternal hematologic levels and pregnancy outcome. *Seminars in Perinatology.* 1981; 5:155–162.

18. Murphy JF, Newcombe RG, O'Riordan J, and Coles EC. Relation of haemoglobin levels in first and second trimesters to outcome of pregnancy. *Lancet.* 1986; 1:992–995.

19. Scholl TO, Hediger ML, Fischer RL, and Shearer JW. Anemia vs iron deficiency: Increased risk of preterm delivery in a prospective study. *American Journal of Clinical Nutrition.* 1992; 55:985–988.

20. CDC criteria for anemia in children and childbearing-aged women. *Morbidity and Mortality Weekly Report.* 1989; 38:400–404.

21. DeMaeyer D and Adiels-Tegman M. The prevalence of anaemia in the world. *World Health Statistics Quarterly.* 1985; 38:302–316.

22. Kim I, Hungerford DW, Yip R, Kuester SA, Zyrkowski C, and Trowbridge FL. Pregnancy nutrition surveillance system—United States, 1979–1990. *Morbidity and Mortality Weekly Report.* 1992; 41: No. SS-7, 25–41.

23. Morck TA, Lynch SR, and Cook JD. Inhibition of food iron absorption by coffee. *American Journal of Clinical Nutrition.* 1983; 37:416–420.

24. Muñoz LM, Lonnerdal B, Keen CL, and Dewey KG. Coffee consumption as a factor in iron-deficiency anemia among pregnant women and their infants in Costa Rica. *American Journal of Clinical Nutrition.* 1988; 48:645–651.

25. Dawson EB, Albers J, and McGanity WJ. Serum zinc changes due to iron supplementation in teenage pregnancy. *American Journal of Clinical Nutrition.* 1989; 50:848–852.

26. Solomons NW. Competitive interaction of iron and zinc in the diet: Consequences for human nutrition. *Journal of Nutrition.* 1986; 116:927–935.

27. Crofton RW, Gvozdanovic D, Gvozdanovic S, Khin CC, Brunt PW, Mowat NAG, and Aggett PJ. Inorganic zinc and the intestinal absorption of ferrous iron. *American Journal of Clinical Nutrition.* 1989; 50:141–144.

28. Sanstrom B, Davidsson L, Cederblad A, and Lonnerdal B. Oral iron, dietary ligands and zinc absorption. *Journal of Nutrition.* 1985; 115:411–414.

29. Food and Nutrition Board, National Academy of Sciences. *Recommended Dietary Allowances.* 10th ed. Washington D.C.: National Academy Press, 1989.

30. Villar J and Repke JT. Calcium supplementation during pregnancy may reduce preterm delivery in high-risk populations. *American Journal of Obstetrics and Gynecology.* 1990; 163:1124–1131.

31. Villar J, Repke JT, Belizan JM, and Pareja G. Calcium supplementation reduces blood pressure during pregnancy: Results of a randomized controlled clinical trial. *Obstetrics and Gynecology.* 1987; 70:317–322.

32. Lopez-Jaramillo P, Narvaez M, Weigel RM, and Yepez R. Calcium supplementation reduces the risk of pregnancy-induced hypertension in an Andes population. *British Journal of Obstetrics and Gynaecology.* 1989; 96:648–655.

33. Marcoux S, Brisson J, and Fabia J. Calcium intake from dairy

products and supplements and the risks of preeclampsia and gestational hypertension. *American Journal of Epidemiology.* 1991; 133:1266–1272.

34. Spatling L and Spatling G. Magnesium supplementation in pregnancy: A double-blind study. *British Journal of Obstetrics and Gynaecology.* 1988; 95:120–125.

35. The People's League of Health. The nutrition of expectant and nursing mothers in relation to maternal and infant mortality and morbidity. *Journal of Obstetrics and Gynaecology of the British Empire.* 1946; 53:498–509.

36. Olsen SF, Hansen HS, Sommer S, et al. Gestational age in relation to marine omega-3 fatty acids in maternal erythrocytes: A study of women in the Faroe Islands and Denmark. *American Journal of Obstetrics and Gynecology.* 1991; 164:1203–1209.

37. Olsen SF and Joensen HD. High liveborn birthweights in the Faroes: Comparison between birthweights in the Faroes and in Denmark. *Journal of Epidemiology and Community Health.* 1985; 39:27–32.

38. Olsen SF, Hansen HS, Sorensen TIA, et al. Intake of marine fat rich in omega-3 polyunsaturated fatty acids may increase birthweight by prolonging gestation. *Lancet.* 1986; 2:367–369.

39. Olsen SF and Secher NJ. A possible preventive effect of low-dose fish oil on early delivery and preeclampsia: Indications from a 50-year-old controlled trial. *British Journal of Nutrition.* 1990; 64:599–609.

40. Scholl TO, Hediger ML, Schall JI, Fischer RL, and Khoo C-S. Low zinc intake during pregnancy: Its association with preterm and very preterm delivery. *American Journal of Epidemiology.* 1993; 137:1115–1124.

41. Recommendations for the use of folic acid to reduce the number of cases of spina bifida and other neural tube defects. *Morbidity and Mortality Weekly Report.* 1992; 41: No. RR–14, 1–7.

42. Bourgoin BP, Evans DR, Cornett JR, Lingard SM, and Quattrone AJ. Lead content in 70 brands of dietary calcium supplements. *American Journal of Public Health.* 1993; 83:1155–1160.

Notes

Chapter 8. The U.S. Laws on Work and Pregnancy

1. National Research Council, Committee on Women's Employment and Related Social Issues. *Work and Family: Policies for a Changing Work Force.* Washington, D.C.: National Academy Press, 1991.
2. U.S. Department of Labor, Women's Bureau. *Maternity Protection of Employed Women.* Bulletin No. 240. Washington, D.C.: U.S. Government Printing Office, 1952; 5–6.

Bibliography

Aslett D and Simons LA. *Make Your House Do the Housework.* Cincinnati, Ohio: Writer's Digest Books, 1986.

Baskette M and Mainella E. *The Art of Nutritional Cooking.* New York: Van Nostrand Reinhold, 1992.

Baxandall R, Gordon L, and Reverby S (eds). *America's Working Women: A Documentary History—1600 to the Present.* New York: Vintage Books/Random House, 1976.

Brazelton TB. *Working and Caring.* Reading, Mass.: Addison-Wesley, 1985.

Brown JE. *Everywoman's Guide to Nutrition.* Minneapolis: University of Minnesota Press, 1991.

Coombs GE, Jr. *The Vitamins: Fundamental Aspects in Nutrition and Health.* San Diego, Calif.: Academic Press, 1992.

Crosby F. *Juggling: The Unexpected Advantages of Balancing Career and Home for Women and Their Families.* New York: The Free Press, 1991.

Davidson MJ and Cooper CL. *Working Women: An International Survey.* Chichester, U.K.: Wiley, 1984.

Frankenhaeuser M, Lundberg U, and Chesney M (eds). *Women, Work, and Health: Stress and Opportunities.* New York: Plenum Press, 1991.

Hamilton M, Kolotkin RL, Cogburn DF, et al. *The Duke University Medical Center Book of Diet and Fitness.* New York: Fawcett Columbine, 1990.

Hess MA and Hunt AE. *Eating for Two—The Complete Guide to Nutrition During Pregnancy.* New York: Collier Books, 1992.

Kamerman SB, Kahn AJ, and Kingston P. *Maternity Policies and Working Women.* New York: Columbia University Press, 1983.

Kenen RH. *Reproductive Hazards in the Workplace: Mending Jobs, Managing Pregnancies.* New York: Harrington Park Press/Haworth Press, 1993.

Kirsta A. *The Book of Stress Survival: Identifying and Reducing the Stress in Your Life.* New York: Fireside Books, 1986.

Luke B, Johnson TRB, and Petrie RH. *Clinical Maternal-Fetal Nutrition.* Boston: Little, Brown, 1993.

Luke B and Keith L. *Principles and Practice of Maternal Nutrition.* London: Parthenon, 1992.

National Research Council. *Work and Family: Policies for a Changing Work Force.* Washington, D.C.: National Academy Press, 1991.

Pennington JAT. *Food Values of Portions Commonly Used.* 16th ed. Philadelphia: JB Lippincott, 1994.

Russell, KP and Niebyl JR. *Eastman's Expectant Motherhood.* 8th ed. Boston: Little, Brown, 1989.

Schofield D. *Confessions of an Organized Homemaker.* Cincinnati, Ohio: Betterway Books, 1994.

Schwartz F. *Breaking with Tradition: Women and Work, the New Facts of Life.* New York: Warner, 1992.

Spodnik JP and Gibbons B. *The 35-plus Diet for Women.* New York: Pocket Books, 1987.

Swinney B. *Eating Expectantly—The Essential Eating Guide and Cookbook for Pregnancy.* Colorado Springs, Colo.: Fall River Press, 1993.

Tilly LA and Scott JW. *Women, Work and Family.* New York: Methuen, 1987.

U.S. Bureau of the Census, Current Population Reports, Series

Bibliography

P–23, No. 165. *Work and Family Patterns of American Women.* Washington, D.C.: Government Printing Office, 1990.

Weisberg AC and Buckler CA. *Everything a Working Mother Needs to Know.* New York: Main Street Books/Doubleday, 1994.

Wertheimer BM. *We Were There: The Story of Working Women in America.* New York: Pantheon Books/Random House, 1977.

Wheatley M and Hirsch MS. *Managing Your Maternity Leave.* New York: Houghton Mifflin, 1983.

Women's Bureau, U.S. Department of Labor. *A Working Woman's Guide to Her Job Rights.* Washington, D.C.: U.S. Department of Labor, 1992.

Index

About the Author

Barbara Luke, Sc.D., M.P.H., R.D., R.N., received her nursing and public health degrees from Columbia University, her degree in nutrition from New York University, and her doctorate in science from Johns Hopkins University. Currently she is an associate professor of obstetrics and gynecology at the University of Michigan Medical School. She is a member of the American College of Obstetricians and Gynecologists, the American Dietetic Association, the American Public Health Association, and the Society of Perinatal Obstetricians. Barbara Luke is the author of eight medical textbooks as well as research and review articles on obstetrics, nutrition, and public health. She lives in Ann Arbor, Michigan.